people's pops

55 recipes for ice pops, shave ice, and boozy pops from brooklyn's coolest pop shop

NATHALIE JORDI, DAVID CARRELL & JOEL HOROWITZ

photography by jennifer may

TEN SPEED PRESS
Berkeley

contents

people's pops

acknowledgments

FOR THEIR GENEROSITY of spirit, brilliant connections, sage counsel, and good humor, we thank Matt Sartwell, Nach Waxman, Rien Fertel, Amanda Hesser, Mitchell Kaplan, John T. Edge, Pableaux Johnson, Brett Martin, Celia Sack, Sara Roahen, Angie Mosier, Ari Weinzweig, and Alex Jordi. The groovy skills of John Goodwin, Robin Hiner, Rue Snider, and Charlie Stopek enabled this business to make technological, aesthetic, and volumetric quantum leaps. Daryl Hanna, Cris and Nadia Gil, Robert LaValva, Colin Alevras, and especially Lucy Watson and Ben Pratt were there to witness—and support—our "social experiment" from the very beginning. Shortly thereafter, Morgan Miller and Katie Myers rained down munificent gifts of time and tube sock: the first winds beneath our wings.

At Ten Speed, Aaron Wehner and Jenny Wapner believed in this book from the get-go; Sara Golski, Jennifer May, Alana Chernila, and Betsy Stromberg made it really beautiful. Eric Johnson generously built us an index. Maya Menendez and Judy Peacock Goodwin, invaluable guides, lovingly keep us on the right side of the law. Alisha Miranda, you don't get your own chapter, but thanks anyway. The Jordi, Carrell, and Horowitz families earn credit for the spectacular support they have provided over the past four (well, thirty) years, as well as the excellent genetics. We also thank Brett Anderson, Danielle Horowitz, and Katie Traynor, who saw the good, the bad, and the ugly and ate many pops without complaint. Finally, we high-five our superb team and terrific customers. You're the reason this is so much fun.

introduction:
the story of people's pops

IN JUNE 2008 our friend Robert LaValva called with an intriguing proposal. He was trying to start a public market for local food producers in New York City. To publicize the cause he was organizing a series of one-day markets, sort of like food flash mobs, and inviting his friends to participate. We were psyched. The only question: what to make?

The only answer: ice pops. Who doesn't love those refreshing little nuggets of fruit and sugar and ice, crystallized summertime? Even industrially produced pops are evocative bites of a common American childhood.

We figured that making pops from local, sustainably grown fruits and herbs and organic sugar had to taste good. Not that we'd ever tried. Over drinks at a bar a friend suggested a name for the experiment:

The People's Popsicle. It sounded good, redolent of a delicious and innocent revolution. Little did we know what would happen next.

Day one: We bought rhubarb, strawberries, cream, blueberries, yogurt, and honey at the Union Square farmers' market.

Day two: We made the pops.

Day three: We sold out in three hours.

Wheels started spinning in all of our brains. A few weeks later we fortuitously saw a flyer advertising the new Brooklyn Flea, a collection of outdoor markets that would soon become legendary as a small business incubator. We began showing up whenever we could swing it, and soon we gathered a loyal following.

Over the following four years we staged pop-up shops in Battery Park, Madison Square Park, and the High Line, opened shops in Chelsea Market and the East Village, and launched a catering business. We appeared on *The Martha Stewart Show*, drove three thousand pops to Chicago for Victoria's Secret, and started selling to Whole Foods. We glued six thousand pop sticks to our shop counter, flooded our kitchen, and received a cease and desist letter from Unilever for improper use of the word *Popsicle*, a trademark that they own. We crashed our van, learned about the properties of biaxially oriented polypropylene, made and sold thousands of pops, and generally had a grand ol' time.

We think our artisanal ice pops have proved popular because they reinvent a well-loved but humble American snack by syncing it with modern values: craftsmanship, the use of sustainably grown ingredients, and a short distance between the fruit on the tree and the consumer.

Also, they're totally delicious!

fundamentals:
fruit + sugar + freeze

ALTHOUGH MAKING POPS is inherently simple, we'd like to share a few lessons we've learned over the years that have greatly improved our production process and made our lives easier. Above all, however, the most important thing to keep in mind is that every piece of fruit in the world is different, and the recipes we've offered are more like guidelines than they are hard-and-fast instructions. Stay relaxed, be creative, and taste every mixture before you pour it into the molds. If the mixture tastes good, the pops will taste good, too.

If you have a question about our recipes, our business, our philosophy, or anything else, feel free to email us (people@peoplespops.com) or stop by one of our shops in Manhattan or Brooklyn. Every one of us in the People's Pops crew spends time in the kitchen making pops, so we should be able to help you with at-home tips, and you might just catch Dave, Nath, or Joel at one of our shops. We'd love it!

notes on fruit

When we first started making pops, our mission was clear: highlight the best fruit we could lay our hands on and support our local economy. We used fruit from the farmers' market to make our first pops and we haven't looked back since. Knowing your farmer means helping your community grow—economically, nutritionally, and deliciously.

That said, although the recipes in this book are organized by season, they'll work at any time of year, with fruit from anywhere. You can even use frozen fruit, as we sometimes have (we buy it from the same local farmers who sell us fresh fruit in season). Keep in mind, though, that with recipes this naked and unadorned, the output will mirror the input. In other words, bland, bloated, flavorless fruit will not materialize into killer pops.

Your best guarantee for flavor-bomb pops? Flavor-bomb fruit, of course.

We find some of the best deals on fruit at farmers' markets. Ask for "seconds," slightly blemished or overripe fruits that may not be beauty pageant material but whose natural sugars and flavors are at their peak. As people who mash fruit for a living, we don't care what the fruit looks like—we're just after flavor. Beauty is in the eye of the beholder, and nothing looks more gorgeous to us than a flat of so-juicy-they're-bursting nectarines.

In the following recipes, we've provided measurements for each fruit in weight and volume. Note, however, that the weight of fruit differs according to how you treat it: washing berries adds weight, while roasting peaches, sieving out seeds from berries, and sloppy spatula work all subtract it. But the most common hazard, in our gluttonous experience, is eating the goods. Since we're incurable tasters, in these recipes we've accounted for the "angel's share," the bit that disappears when no one is paying

attention. That said, making pops isn't like baking: the measurements we've provided are guidelines rather than written in stone. Your taste buds are the ultimate arbiters of balance and flavor.

flavor combinations

People often ask how we come up with ideas for flavors. It's simple: when ice pops dominate your world, as they do ours, you start seeing new applications everywhere—in cocktails, in desserts, and in jams. Our peach-bourbon pop is a riff on a julep; the strawberry–balsamic vinegar pop is an adaptation of an Italian dessert.

We also know that what grows together goes together, and strolling through the market sizing up ingredients is another way we've come up with many of our best flavor combinations—the apricot and lavender in July, and the nectarine, chamomile, and honey in August.

We sometimes find ourselves categorizing fruits, herbs, and spices as either "warm" or "cool." "Warm" fruits, we believe, often pair well with other "warm" ingredients, and the same is true for "cool" fruits and ingredients. For example, when we discovered that we liked the combination of apricot and caramel, we figured that rhubarb and caramel would probably

warm fruit

rhubarb
pumpkin
pear
apple
peach
apricot

warm ingredient

caramel
cardamom
chamomile
cinnamon
cream
honey
star anise
vanilla
bourbon
cognac

cool fruit

cucumber
grape
watermelon
cantaloupe
tomato

cool ingredient

basil
ginger
hyssop
mint
shiso
tarragon
vodka
gin

also taste wonderful (it did). Above are examples of some "warm" and "cool" fruits and other ingredients, in case you want to try mixing and matching them on your own. You like the idea of our watermelon and lemongrass pop but only have ginger in the house? Make it with ginger, then—it'll be just as tasty.

Of course, this categorization isn't definitive. Many fruits work with both warm and cool ingredients (berries are famously ambidextrous), and some fruits that favor one side can be beautifully paired with ingredients on the other (apple and mint is a classic example).

simple syrup

We use simple syrup to sweeten our pops, because the natural sweetness of fruit tends to fade when you freeze it. Simple syrup is nothing more than sugar dissolved in an equal quantity of water by heating it.

We've experimented with many different sweeteners, eventually settling on organic cane sugar. These are large grains of amber-colored sugar, the result of dehydrating cane syrup (often labeled as "dehydrated cane syrup" in stores), easily found at retailers such as Whole Foods. But you can also substitute other sweeteners, such as granulated white sugar, agave nectar, or honey, any of which works fine. Just remember that they all manifest slightly different flavors and degrees of sweetness, so you'll have to adjust the mixture to taste.

The basic simple syrup recipe is $^2/_3$ cup (5 fl oz) water + $^2/_3$ cup (5 oz) sugar = 1 cup (8 fl oz) simple syrup. This recipe can easily be scaled up or down—just remember that for every volume of simple syrup you want to make, you'll need 62.5 percent of that amount of both water and sugar. So, for example, if you want to end up with $1^1/_4$ cups simple syrup, combine $^3/_4$ cup water ($1^1/_4$ cups x .625) with $^3/_4$ cup sugar ($1^1/_4$ cups x .625). If you end up with extra simple syrup, there are tons of uses for it, including sweetening your coffee, tea, or cocktails.

Many of the herbs and spices we use in our pops are introduced by heating them in simple syrup so that their flavors infuse the syrup. The herbs or spices can then be strained out or left in, depending on your preference. We've found that in the amount of time it takes to properly infuse an herb or a spice into simple syrup, about 15 percent of the syrup evaporates, which our recipes take into account. Remember that the longer you cook your simple syrup the more it will reduce, which means that if you overboil your simple syrup, you may end up short. So keep an eye on the stove.

Add simple syrup to your pop mixture a bit at a time and taste as you go, because it's hard to rewind once you've gone overboard. Lemon juice or other acidic ingredients will somewhat offset excessive sweetness, but it's better to be careful the first time around. That said, as a rule of thumb you'll want your mixtures to taste slightly too sweet, because their sweetness will be dulled when the mixture is frozen. On the flip side, too much sugar (or alcohol) in your pops will keep them from freezing. As with everything in life, moderation is the key.

Although the temperature of your simple syrup won't affect the end result of the pops per se, keep in mind that simple syrup that's warmer will taste sweeter, and syrup that's colder will taste less sweet. That means if you add warm syrup to your fruit mixture, you'll need to add a little more than you might think, because you'll be tricked into thinking you've added enough when you haven't yet.

Making an infused simple syrup is a great way to use up wilting herbs. Instead of throwing out the shriveled-up mint or basil in your fridge, preserve their flavor by infusing them into syrup, either separately or together. You'll be halfway to a batch of ice pops already!

Although you can combine several flavors of leftover syrup to delicious effect (using black tea and

simple syrup

²/₃ cup (5 oz) **organic cane sugar**
²/₃ cup (5 fl oz) **water**

Combine the sugar and water in a small saucepan and bring to a simmer over medium-high heat, stirring until the sugar dissolves and the mixture is transparent. Turn off the heat and let cool. Add any spices before the mixture starts to simmer; add any herbs only after you've turned off the heat. Store plain and infused syrups in sealed containers in the fridge.

MAKES 1 CUP (8 FL OZ)

cardamom syrup, for example), always label all of the ingredients in your syrup. With the number of serious food allergies around these days, you can't play it too safe.

Plain and infused simple syrups last for weeks, or even months. Just be sure to refrigerate them, particularly if they have been infused with perishables like herbs or tea. (See the photo of simple syrup infused with star anise and vanilla at left.)

booze in pops

We're not allowed to sell boozy pops at our stands, but we've made plenty for our own delectable consumption at home. Given that alcohol inhibits freezing, avoid composing a pop with more than 20 percent booze, or it won't freeze well and may break in half upon unmolding. But we love the softer texture that booze imparts to pops, so feel free to amend any of the nonalcoholic pops in this book to include some type of spirit (see the table of "warm" and "cool" ingredients on page 5 for some ideas).

We have had limited success incorporating carbonated beverages into our pops. Having experimented with artisanal sodas, Champagne, and other fizzy drinks, we find that the carbonation lends the pop a mild but bizarre sour taste. It's too bad, because don't strawberry and Champagne pops sound absolutely delicious?

live and learn

The following are some of the tips and techniques we've learned in our years of making pops. Mostly the hard way.

- When making small batches of pops, such as the ones in this book, we like to use a 1-quart Pyrex measuring cup with a pouring spout. The measurement lines make it easy to add ingredients in the correct amount, and the spout makes pouring pops into the mold easy and efficient. There's less cleanup afterward, too, and less mixture lost in various bowls due to sloppy spatula work.

- When puréeing small quantities of hard-to-purée ingredients such as fennel, celery, or corn, we find it helpful to add a bit of simple syrup or water. Just remember to account for the fact later, and adjust the amount of simple syrup accordingly.

- Whether to strain out an ingredient's seeds, skin, or fibers depends entirely on your personal preference. We find that straining gives some ingredients (especially vegetables) a softer, more crowd-pleasing texture and ramps up a pop's level of sophistication. Although we do strain out the tough skins of fruits such as grapes and blueberries, we almost always leave in the thin, flavorful, nuance-giving skins of stone fruits such as peaches, plums, and apricots. Whether or not we get rid of berry seeds depends on how much time we have and how we're feeling. Leaving them in yields a rustic texture, straining them out a more refined one. Both taste fantastic. When straining seeds we find that it's faster and easier to mix the syrup into the puréed berries first and *then* strain the seeds; the added liquid helps the juices pass through the sieve more easily.

- There is a major difference in flavor between freshly squeezed lemon juice and bottled lemon juice, the former tasting infinitely better in the finished product, the latter tasting canned. If you like shortcuts, fine, so do we. Just don't use this one.

- One final and very important note. Fruit is not standardized; it invariably fluctuates in ripeness, sweetness, size, and texture, even if the pieces are from the same tree. Use our recipes as a guideline, but your mouth should be the ultimate judge of sweetness and balance. *Always* taste before you pour the pops into the molds (that's part of the fun, remember?) and adjust the mixture accordingly.

molds and freezing

During our first three years in business we used plastic ice pop molds we bought from Amazon.com to make thousands upon thousands of pops. The molds had ten cavities, each $2^1/_2$ ounces.

We used these same molds to test the recipes in this book. Consequently, each recipe yields ten $2^1/_2$-ounce pops, or approximately $3^1/_8$ cups (25 fl oz) of mixture before pouring. But you don't need fancy molds to make pops: they can also be made in small paper cups, shot glasses, stainless steel molds, ice cube trays—the sky's the limit. Just remember that wide pops are hard to wrap your mouth around, and that unmolding pops is easier when the molds are somewhat tapered (wider at the end where the stick comes out). And the bigger the pop, the longer it will take to freeze.

Although we have now graduated to using specialized stainless steel molds that sit in a hypercooled alcohol bath and freeze pops in 18 minutes, you can use a regular freezer to turn out absolutely delicious

pops, like we did for our first three years in business. You can also purchase a fast-freeze home pop maker like the one made by Zoku, which is available online and at some kitchen supply stores. However, keep in mind that the faster the mixture freezes the smaller the ice crystals will be, which leads to a creamier texture and a longer shelf life, so turn your freezer to its coldest setting, place the pops in the back near the bottom, where the freezer is coldest, and avoid opening the freezer door while the pops are freezing.

Mixtures, especially those with a high liquid content, expand upon freezing, so leave a small space, approximately ¹/₄ inch, at the top of each mold to avoid overflow. If your molds come with lids, you can add the sticks immediately, holding them in place with paperclips if they threaten to slip down. If they don't, freeze the mixture for 1 to 2 hours, until a stick placed in it will stay upright.

Striped pops are awfully pretty, though they take a little more work. (They're also a great way to put to work any bits of mixture you have left over.) To achieve this look, pour whatever flavor you want at the tip of the pop into the bottom of the mold and freeze until solid, 2 to 3 hours, then add the next layer, and so on. Remember that to be of any use the stick needs a couple of inches of real estate in the pop, so plan your architecture accordingly.

unmolding and storage

To unmold your pops, fill a sink with lots of hot water. If your mold has a top, take it off now. Carefully dip the mold into the water so that the whole pop is submerged but the water doesn't get the pop wet by flowing over the top of the mold. Hold it in the water for a few seconds and then tug carefully on the stick. If the pop doesn't come out easily, it

needs to be submerged again. Make sure the water goes all the way up to where the pop stops. If it doesn't, you'll be melting the bottom half of the pop while tugging hopelessly at the frozen top half.

Store the pops in small, airtight resealable plastic bags in the freezer. Because our recipes do not include any preservatives, stabilizers, or emulsifiers, some degree of freezer burn (dehydration due to moisture's inexorable migration to the surface) will start setting in after a few weeks. Good storage will slow this natural process. Kept in sealed plastic bags, our pops will keep for months. Not wanting to add more plastic to the world's landfills, we have experimented with corn-based biodegradable packaging, but unfortunately we have found that its porosity (a precondition for biodegradation) hastens the freezer burn we are trying so hard to avoid. We are keeping our ears peeled for a better solution, but in the meantime we are back to using plastic.

serving suggestions

Remember that if you want to serve pops at a party, you'll have to keep them cold all the way from the freezer to the eater. We rely heavily on dry ice: 5 pounds of it should keep the pops frozen for a couple of hours.

We love to serve pops in a stainless steel bucket with dry ice at the bottom and cubed ice on top. You can lodge the pops attractively between the ice cubes, but be sure not to touch the dry ice with your bare hands—it's dangerous stuff! Another suggestion is to serve the pops alongside some of the fruit or herbs from which they are made.

We've made thousands of pops the exact same way you would at home: shopping at the farmers' market, using very simple ingredients, preparing fruit in small batches, and using molds you can buy at many stores. But remember: these recipes are just guidelines. The sweetness, size, and ripeness of the fruit you buy will dictate your final result more than our recipe does. So trust your instincts. Fiddle with the proportions until your mixture tastes good. And *enjoy*!

spring

RHUBARB
rhubarb & jasmine | 17

rhubarb & elderflower | 19

rhubarb & strawberry | 20

STRAWBERRIES
straight-up strawberry | 21

strawberries & cream | 22

strawberries & balsamic vinegar | 23

strawberries & bitters | 24

CUCUMBERS
cucumber & violet | 25

cucumber, elderflower & tequila | 26

WE SPEND SO MUCH TIME over the winter revving back up for warmer weather that it's a relief when spring finally arrives and we find ourselves back in the kitchen.

Sometimes, when it's hot outside but the fruit on the trees hasn't yet ripened, we begin the season by using frozen fruit. It comes from the same farms as our fresh fruit, so we know the source. Some frozen fruits work really well. Rhubarb, berries, and fruits that don't mind stewing, such as pears or plums, come to mind. (Melons? Forget about it.)

The fastest way to defrost fruit is to fill the sink with cold water and place the container with the frozen fruit in the water. Be careful, however, that the fruit itself doesn't get wet.

. . . .

rhubarb

If we had a nickel for every time we've explained what rhubarb is to someone, we could probably afford to quit the ice pop racket. What we tell people is that it looks like pink celery, and though it's technically a vegetable, in 1947 a New York court decided that because rhubarb is predominantly used the way fruits are, it was eligible to be considered as such for purposes of taxation and regulation (a better deal for the rhubarb farmers).

Rhubarb beats out all of the season's other fruits in showing up at the market, and we get really excited when we see its elegant pink-and-green stalks cozying up to the greens and ponderous root vegetables of late winter. It's compatible with an incredible variety of flavors and cooks down beautifully into a mellow purée that hardly needs further processing. Once you've tried the recipes in this chapter, think of combining rhubarb with almond, cardamom, gingerbread, juniper, lavender, orange blossom, or white tea.

We cook rhubarb down until it is completely soft yet still holds together. You should be able to see clearly defined stalks in the mixture that gently fall apart when touched. These bits provide a lovely texture and visual appeal.

strawberries

We're always extremely excited to see strawberries arrive at the farmers' markets, but by mid-June, when we're suffering from whatever the equivalent of carpal tunnel syndrome is that one gets from hulling strawberries, we're even more psyched to see them go. Of course, as soon as they're gone, then we miss them.

Strawberries are incredibly variable in flavor, so seek out the freshest, most delicious ones. Water-bloated, flavorless strawberries will inevitably lead to icy, flavorless pops. Choose only berries that are fully red, keep them out of the sun, and use them soon after purchasing them. Wash them quickly in cold water (don't let them soak), and drain them well before hulling them. Strawberries benefit from a touch of lemon juice to prop up their weak natural acidity.

In addition to the flavor combinations recommended here, consider pairing strawberries with violet, buttermilk, Cognac, tequila, or anything else that suits your fancy.

cucumbers

On a really hot day a cucumber pop is an unparalleled instrument of refreshment. Although cukes freeze quite icily, the hotter the weather, the more what is technically a flaw will morph into a benefit.

It may seem unusual to use a vegetable in dessert, but cucumbers belong to the same plant family as melons, and they can be used to much the same effect in ice pops: the mild and slightly sweet flavor lends itself well to further sweetening and acts as a blank slate for showcasing other ingredients. Flavors to consider pairing with cucumber include fennel, ginger, honey, hyssop, mint, vodka, and yogurt.

A raw cucumber should feel firm when gently squeezed. Whether to peel or seed the cukes is up to you. Generally, we opt to peel but not seed them, because seeding nearly halves the volume of each cucumber and the seeds seem to vanish when the mixture is thoroughly puréed anyway. Given cucumbers' lack of natural acidity, a touch of lemon juice helps the flavors sparkle.

rhubarb & jasmine

The "jasminey-ness" of the finished pop is entirely dictated by the type and amount of jasmine you use. We base our judgment on the jasmine's aroma: very fragrant jasmine requires only three to five pearls, whereas faint-smelling jasmine might need ten to fifteen. A minute or so after you drop the pearls into the simmering simple syrup, waft some of the steam your way. If an energetic aroma of jasmine fills your nostrils, stop there. If not, add more jasmine until it does. Jasmine also pairs beautifully with blackberries, pears, and apricots. | MAKES 10 POPS

1¹/₂ cups (12 fl oz) simple syrup (page 7)

3 to 15 pearls jasmine tea (see above)

1 pound rhubarb (about 5 long stalks), trimmed and chopped
into 1-inch pieces

Heat the simple syrup in a covered saucepan over medium-high heat. Somewhere between a simmer and a full boil, turn off the heat and add the jasmine tea pearls, which should promptly unfurl as you stir briefly. Be careful not to simmer the mixture for too long, because the simple syrup evaporates quickly, reducing the amount of liquid remaining. You want 1 cup plus 2 tablespoons (9 fl oz) to work with. If, after 1 minute, the smell of jasmine is not pronounced, add more jasmine. It's a really subtle flavor and has a habit of hiding under the rhubarb, so make sure it's really present in the simple syrup to begin with. Steep for 10 minutes and then strain out the jasmine, pressing down on the flowers to extract as much liquid as possible. Let cool. Can you still smell it? If not, add more and reboil. Jasmine is subtle!

Pour about ¹/₂ inch of water into a shallow, heavy, nonreactive saucepan and add the chopped rhubarb. Cook over medium heat, stirring frequently to make sure the rhubarb doesn't stick to the bottom of the pan and burn, until the pieces have mostly dissolved into a thick and gloppy

continued

purée, 10 to 15 minutes. Pick out and discard any bits that are still stringy (there shouldn't be many; if there are, keep cooking until the rhubarb breaks down some more). Stir the mixture to smooth it out (but it doesn't have to be entirely homogenous). You should have about 2 cups plus 2 tablespoons (17 fl oz) of purée.

Transfer the rhubarb purée into a bowl or measuring pitcher with a pouring spout, add the jasmine simple syrup, and stir well to combine. Taste; the mixture should be quite sweet and the jasmine flavor subtle but noticeable. Adjust to taste.

Pour the mixture into your ice pop molds, leaving a little bit of room at the top for the mixture to expand. Insert sticks and freeze until solid, 4 to 5 hours. Unmold and transfer to plastic bags for storage or serve at once.

DISPATCH FROM THE FIELD

While the summer's fruit is still just budding on branches, we are already busy preparing for the season. We get our worker's comp set up, touch base with the Department of Agriculture & Markets, and pick up the keys to Chelsea Market. We argue over how to display our pops in the five-foot freezer case and discuss the pros and cons of using an iPad as our cash register. We order ingredients like thyme, ginger beer, orange blossom water, and elderflower syrup. We pick up stools, paint, and stamp pop sticks. This is the most frenzied part of our season, and for everything that gets accomplished, two more things to do pop up. It's like playing that arcade game where moles pop out of holes and you have to punch them back in, and as you slowly get the hang of it, the moles start coming faster and faster until you *lose your mind*.

rhubarb & elderflower

This flavor combo, a real harbinger of spring, is one of the first pops we make each season. The foamy-looking, fragrant flowers of the elder tree bloom at around the same time of the year as rhubarb, for those inclined to make their own cordial or syrup, but bottled elderflower syrup can readily be found online and at some gourmet grocers and liquor stores (we look for the Monin brand). This recipe also works fine with frozen rhubarb, which can be cooked in the same way as raw. | MAKES 10 POPS

1 pound rhubarb (about 5 long stalks), trimmed and chopped
into 1-inch pieces
$^2/_3$ cup (5 fl oz) simple syrup (page 7)
$^1/_3$ cup (3 fl oz) elderflower syrup

Pour about $^1/_2$ inch of water into a shallow, heavy, nonreactive saucepan and add the rhubarb. Cook over medium heat, stirring frequently to make sure the rhubarb doesn't stick to the bottom of the pan and burn, until the pieces have mostly dissolved into a thick and gloppy purée, 10 to 15 minutes. Pick out and discard any bits that are still stringy (there shouldn't be many; if there are, keep cooking until the rhubarb breaks down some more). Stir the mixture to smooth it out (but it doesn't have to be entirely homogenous). You should have about 2 cups plus 2 tablespoons (17 fl oz) of purée.

Pour the purée into a bowl or measuring pitcher with a pouring spout, add the simple syrup and elderflower syrup, and stir well to combine. Taste; the mixture should be quite sweet, with a marked lemony-elderflower flavor. Adjust if necessary.

Pour the mixture into your ice pop molds, leaving a little bit of room at the top for the mixture to expand. Insert sticks and freeze until solid, 4 to 5 hours. Unmold and transfer to plastic bags for storage or serve at once.

rhubarb & strawberry

The gateway to other rhubarb combinations is often this pop, probably because most people associate rhubarb with strawberry-rhubarb pie. There's no question that it's a great match, especially in the early dawn of springtime, when strawberries are too scarce to be used alone. | MAKES 10 POPS

^{1}/$_2$ pound rhubarb (2 to 3 stalks), trimmed and chopped into 1-inch pieces

10 ounces (2^1/$_2$ cups) strawberries, hulled

1 cup (8 fl oz) simple syrup (page 7)

2 tablespoons (1 fl oz) freshly squeezed lemon juice

Pour about ^{1}/$_2$ inch of water into a shallow, heavy, nonreactive saucepan and add the chopped rhubarb. Cook over medium heat, stirring frequently to make sure the rhubarb doesn't stick to the bottom of the pan and burn, until the pieces have mostly dissolved into a thick and gloppy purée, about 10 minutes. Pick out and discard any bits that are still stringy (there shouldn't be many; if there are, keep cooking until the rhubarb breaks down some more). Stir the mixture to smooth it out (but it doesn't have to be entirely homogenous). You should have about 1 cup (8 fl oz) of purée.

Purée the strawberries in a food processor. You should have about 1 cup (8 fl oz) of purée.

In a bowl or measuring pitcher with a pouring spout, combine the strawberry and rhubarb purées and simple syrup. Stir well to combine and taste; the mixture should be quite sweet and taste of both rhubarb and strawberries. Adjust to taste.

Pour the mixture into your ice pop molds, leaving a little bit of room at the top for the mixture to expand. Insert sticks and freeze until solid, 4 to 5 hours. Unmold and transfer to plastic bags for storage or serve at once.

straight-up strawberry

The simplest pop in this book is nonetheless just as delicious as some of the more sophisticated ones, although the texture tends to be somewhat icy. Using frozen strawberries exacerbates this problem, so use fresh if you can find them. It goes without saying that in a recipe this naked, the better the berries, the better the pop. | MAKES 10 POPS

Just over 1 pound (4 cups) strawberries, hulled
3/4 cup plus 2 tablespoons (7 fl oz) simple syrup (page 7)
2 tablespoons (1 fl oz) freshly squeezed lemon juice

Purée the strawberries in a food processor. You should have about 2 cups (16 fl oz) of purée.

Transfer the puréed strawberries to a bowl or measuring pitcher with a pouring spout and add the simple syrup and lemon juice. Stir well to combine and taste; the mixture should be quite sweet and taste bright. Adjust as necessary.

Pour the mixture into your ice pop molds, leaving a little bit of room at the top for the mixture to expand. Insert sticks and freeze until solid, 4 to 5 hours. Unmold and transfer to plastic bags for storage or serve at once.

strawberries & cream

Cream does a lot to improve a pop's texture, so this classic Wimbledon combination is a real crowd-pleaser. You can mix in the cream as thoroughly or as little as you like, according to what looks best to you. We like to make sure the strawberries and cream are well mixed but still look marbled. For a delicious variation, use buttermilk instead of cream, but if you do so, change the proportions to 1²/3 cups (13 fl oz) puréed strawberries, 2/3 cup (5 fl oz) simple syrup, and 3/4 cup plus 2 tablespoons (7 fl oz) buttermilk. **| MAKES 10 POPS**

Just over 1 pound (4 cups) strawberries, hulled
3/4 cup plus 2 tablespoons (7 fl oz) simple syrup (page 7)
1/4 cup (2 fl oz) heavy cream
1 tablespoon freshly squeezed lemon juice, if needed

Purée the strawberries in a food processor. You should have about 2 cups (16 fl oz) of purée.

Transfer the puréed strawberries to a bowl or measuring pitcher with a pouring spout and add the simple syrup. Stir well to combine. Add the cream and mix according to your aesthetic preference. Taste; the mixture should be sweet and mouth-fillingly creamy but not cloying. Adjust to taste, adding the lemon juice if the mixture tastes a little flat.

Pour the mixture into your ice pop molds, leaving a little bit of room at the top for the mixture to expand. Insert sticks and freeze until solid, 4 to 5 hours. Unmold and transfer to plastic bags for storage or serve at once.

strawberries & balsamic vinegar

This recipe was inspired by the Italian practice of pouring aged balsamic vinegar over strawberries for dessert. When balsamic vinegar is made in the traditional manner, this extraordinary condiment (a reduction of grape juice) is subsequently aged in different barrels that get smaller and smaller as the liquid evaporates and the flavor intensifies. We first tried making this recipe using copious quantities of precious twenty-year-old aged balsamic, which was like flushing money down a toilet. All the subtlety of the syrupy vinegar was lost. Our second batch, made using supermarket balsamic vinegar, was much better—and less expensive. Consider combining balsamic vinegar with cranberries or figs, too. | MAKES 10 POPS

Just over 1 pound (4 cups) strawberries, hulled

3/4 cup (6 fl oz) simple syrup (page 7)

1 tablespoon freshly squeezed lemon juice

1/4 cup (2 fl oz) balsamic vinegar, or more if needed

Purée the strawberries in a food processor. You should have about 2 cups (16 fl oz) of purée.

Transfer the puréed strawberries to a bowl or measuring pitcher with a pouring spout and add the simple syrup and lemon juice. Stir well to combine. Taste; the mixture should be sweet and brightly flavored. Add the balsamic vinegar bit by bit, stirring well to combine and tasting as you go. Do you notice the sweet and sour twinge the vinegar has added?

The intensity of balsamic vinegar can vary, so add a bit more if necessary, but be careful: a little goes a long way.

Pour the mixture into your ice pop molds, leaving a little bit of room at the top for the mixture to expand. Insert sticks and freeze until solid, 4 to 5 hours. Unmold and transfer to plastic bags for storage or serve at once.

strawberries & bitters

We came up with this wonderfully quirky flavor while raiding the liquor cabinet to see what might taste delicious in a strawberry pop. Bartenders usually use only a dash or two of Angostura bitters in a cocktail, but we love the flavor, so we piled it on here. You need to use a much heavier hand than you would when making a drink or the flavor will drown under the weight of the strawberry. Feel free to experiment with other kinds of bitters, such as Peychaud's or your own homemade variety. Alternatively, pair bitters with pears, plums, or even tomatoes. | MAKES 10 POPS

1 pound 2 ounces (4¹/₂ cups) strawberries, hulled
³/₄ cup (6 fl oz) simple syrup (page 7)
2 tablespoons (1 fl oz) freshly squeezed lemon juice
1¹/₂ to 2 tablespoons (³/₄ to 1 fl oz) Angostura bitters

Purée the strawberries in a food processor. You should have about 2 cups plus 2 tablespoons (17 fl oz) of purée.

Transfer the puréed strawberries to a bowl or measuring pitcher with a pouring spout and add the simple syrup and lemon juice. Stir well to combine. Taste; at this point the mixture should be both sweet and bright. The exact amounts of simple syrup and lemon juice needed will vary depending on the intrinsic sweetness of the strawberries. Add the Angostura bitters bit by bit until you can taste them definitively, but stop before the mixture becomes excessively bitter.

Pour the mixture into your ice pop molds, leaving a little bit of room at the top for the mixture to expand. Insert sticks and freeze until solid, 4 to 5 hours. Unmold and transfer to plastic bags for storage or serve at once.

cucumber & violet

This pop sounds kind of bizarre, but it tastes better than you'd expect, or at least we think so. Like all the cuke pops, it's better than water on a hot day. Add the violet bit by bit, because its potency will depend on whether you use syrup, extract, or essence, and if you add too much, you'll end up with a pop that tastes like potpourri. This pop is also outstanding made with strawberries instead of cucumber. Use $2^{1}/_3$ cups (19 fl oz) puréed strawberries, $1/_2$ cup (4 fl oz) simple syrup, and $1/_4$ cup (2 fl oz) violet syrup. You can find violet syrup online, in baking supply stores, and in some liquor stores, where, if so inspired, you could also experiment with crème de violette. | MAKES 10 POPS

$1^{1}/_4$ pounds cucumbers (2 large or 3 small), peeled
$2/_3$ cup (5 fl oz) simple syrup (page 7)
2 tablespoons (1 fl oz) freshly squeezed lemon juice
$1/_4$ cup (2 fl oz) violet syrup, extract, or essence

Finely purée the cucumbers in a food processor. You should have about 2 cups plus 2 tablespoons (17 fl oz) of purée.

Transfer the puréed cucumbers to a bowl or measuring pitcher with a pouring spout and add the simple syrup and lemon juice. Add the violet syrup bit by bit, tasting as you go. Stop when the violet flavor becomes pronounced but not overwhelming.

Pour the mixture into your ice pop molds, leaving a little bit of room at the top for the mixture to expand. Insert sticks and freeze until solid, 4 to 5 hours. Unmold and transfer to plastic bags for storage or serve at once.

cucumber, elderflower & tequila

Incredibly sophisticated but satisfying, too—this pop will rock your world. It's got these great bones made up of cucumber and elderflower—two really clean, wholesome flavors—but the tequila gives it a dirty, spicy edge. The texture is schizophrenic, too: cucumber freezes icily, elderflower gives it a buttery edge, and tequila softens the whole thing. This pop is a real party for your mouth, if you like that kind of thing. We do. | MAKES 10 POPS

$1^1/3$ pounds cucumbers (about 3 medium), peeled

$^1/3$ cup (3 fl oz) elderflower syrup

2 tablespoons (1 fl oz) freshly squeezed lemon juice

$^1/4$ to $^1/3$ cup (2 to 3 fl oz) tequila

Finely purée the cucumbers in a food processor. You should have about $2^1/2$ cups (20 fl oz) of purée.

Transfer the puréed cucumbers to a bowl or measuring pitcher with a pouring spout and stir in the elderflower syrup and lemon juice, and then the tequila. Taste and adjust, but be careful not to overdo the tequila, because too much will keep the pop from freezing.

Pour the mixture into your ice pop molds, leaving a little bit of room at the top for the mixture to expand. Insert sticks and freeze until solid, 4 to 5 hours. Unmold and transfer to plastic bags for storage or serve at once.

early summer

BLUEBERRIES

blueberry & buttermilk | 33

blueberry & cardamom | 34

blueberry moonshine | 37

RASPBERRIES

straight-up raspberry | 38

raspberries & basil | 39

raspberries & cream | 40

raspberry jam & yogurt | 42

SOUR CHERRIES

sour cherry & almond | 43

BLACKBERRIES

blackberry & rose | 45

blackberry, yogurt & honey | 46

blackberry & lemon verbena | 47

AH, BERRIES. Has there ever been a more perfect fruit for ice pops? They don't need to be seeded, stoned, peeled, hulled, or pitted (except for cherries), and they have a built-in acidity that translates into pops with a really well-balanced flavor. After hulling a gazillion strawberries, we breathe a big sigh of relief when the blueberries come in.

Berries have an incredibly short shelf life, which means you can often get a great deal on them at farmers' markets. Think of the end of Seamus Heaney's wonderful poem "Blackberry Picking":

> *It wasn't fair*
> *That all the lovely canfuls smelt of rot.*
> *Each year I hoped they'd keep, knew they would not.*

Somebody send this man our Blackberry & Rose recipe!

blueberries

Of all the fruits we use, blueberries are one of the friendliest. In the sink, they descend gently to the bottom while the stems and leaves float to the surface, where they can be picked out easily, and they don't absorb water the way softer berries do. They don't need pitting, hulling, or peeling. Whether or not they need to be sieved is a matter of contention between Nathalie, who thinks that they do, and Joel, who thinks that they don't. Not sieving blueberries will result in a textured pop punctuated with crispy little seeds, which tend to sink to the bottom of the mold, or the tip of the pop. Sieving is a bit of a struggle and will result in your losing about 15 to 20 percent of the fruit, but it's good exercise and your efforts will be rewarded with incredibly soft texture and rich flavor.

Although most fruits lose sweetness when frozen into pops, freezing seems to magnify blueberries' sweetness, so don't overdo it. We also recommend using freshly squeezed lemon juice in blueberry pops, because it counters blueberries' natural lack of acidity.

In addition to the examples in this chapter, consider pairing blueberries with citrus, cream, lavender, or black tea.

raspberries

Of all the fruits out there, raspberries may be those best suited to making pops. They have a natural acidity that really comes to life upon freezing, and their texture is unparalleled. You can strain out the seeds for a more refined texture, but we like the rustic feel and interesting crunch of the seeds. To avoid the bland taste of waterlogged fruit, try to use raspberries that have dried off thoroughly after being washed. Frozen raspberries work quite well, although if you heat them up as part of the defrosting process, like we do, they will take on a jammy taste. It's noticeably different, but no less delicious.

The best pop we think we've ever made—Raspberries & Basil (page 39)—is in this chapter, but consider pairing raspberries with star anise, vanilla, white tea, or bergamot as well.

sour cherries

One morning at the Union Square Greenmarket we were introduced to Peter Hoffman, the legendary New York City chef who was one of the first to make shopping there cool. "Hey, you should put these sour cherries into your pops," he said. No way, we thought. We'd been burned by cherries before. Our one previ-

ous attempt had involved an entire afternoon of pitting, followed by an unfortunate puréeing that turned the cherries an unappealing brown and dissipated all of their flavor. "Not these," said Peter. "Cook them with sugar, like you would to make jam. The color's amazing and the taste will blow your mind."

When the likes of Peter Hoffman gives you these pearls of wisdom, you listen. You buy. You stem the cherries, watch them ripple like expensive marbles as you pour them into a big jam pot, add some organic sugar, and turn on the heat. He was right. Piquant and full-flavored, they turned a gorgeous ruby red. Our one mistake? Figuring that the cooked cherries would burst like damson plums, releasing their pits buoyantly to the top of the pot. Boy, did we figure wrong.

What transpired were four hours of Nathalie hunting down cherry pits while Joel hulled, puréed, strained, mixed, poured, froze, cleaned up, and laughed at her. And when we say Nathalie was pitting cherries, what we mean is that she was wading through a heaving morass of cherry corpses picking out a thousand little nuggets of a lawsuit waiting to happen. "Can't we leave some in here?" she asked Joel. "Like the golden ticket in *Charlie and the Chocolate Factory*. First person to find one wins a prize."

"Like what?" he retorted. "The Heimlich Maneuver?"

The pops were delicious, but we swore we were never going through that again. Fortunately, we can now buy pitted cherries from a local supplier. If you're only making a small quantity of pops, though, just pit them yourself.

If you can't find fresh or frozen sour cherries, use canned or jarred pitted Montmorency cherries. Don't bother making pops with sweet or Bing cherries. They will oxidize, become an ugly vomitous brown, lose all their flavor, and waste all your time. We recommend puréeing pure cherry mixtures finely, to avoid shardy outcomes, but consider dropping whole sour cherries in with other puréed fruit. For example, our plum and sour cherry pops, in which rich puréed plums are studded with tart whole sour cherries, are really popular. In addition to the flavors mentioned here, we recommend pairing cherries with kirsch, violet, rum, ginger, or bitters.

blackberries

One of the most elusive of all the soft fruits, blackberries have a short season and a high price, so it's a real luxury when we get to work with them. It doesn't help that fresh blackberries are so irresistible that half of them disappear down our gullets before they have a chance to graduate to ice pops. Oh, the occupational hazards!

One disadvantage of blackberries is that they have a very short shelf life and consequently should be used as soon as possible after purchasing. One advantage, however, is that they work equally well with both "warm" and "cool" ingredients (see page 5). Try pairing blackberries with citrus, cream, jasmine, or violet. A touch of lemon juice will brighten blackberry's acidity, but it isn't essential.

We find that it's faster to fully mix any syrups and seasonings you're using into the puréed berries before straining them. The added liquid helps the blackberry juice pass through the strainer more easily.

blueberry & buttermilk

Blueberries and cream are a real crowd-pleaser, but we've elected to give you a slight variation on the theme. If you want to make the original, the proportions are 2⅓ cups (19 fl oz) puréed blueberries, ½ cup (4 fl oz) simple syrup, ¼ cup (2 fl oz) heavy cream, and 2 tablespoons (1 fl oz) lemon juice. As with all blueberry pops, whether or not you want to strain out the skins and seeds is up to you and how much time and energy you can muster, but we think straining is worth the effort. Buttermilk also pairs well with strawberries, rhubarb, and pears.   MAKES 10 POPS

1 pound 2 ounces (4 cups) blueberries
⅔ cup (5 fl oz) simple syrup (page 7)
2 tablespoons (1 fl oz) freshly squeezed lemon juice
½ cup (4 fl oz) buttermilk

Pick out any stems or leaves from the blueberries and purée them in a food processor. You should have about 1¾ cups plus 2 tablespoons (15 fl oz) of purée.

Combine the puréed blueberries, simple syrup, and lemon juice in a bowl or measuring pitcher with a pouring spout. Taste; the precise amount of simple syrup and lemon juice needed will depend on how sweet the berries were to begin with. Be aware that blueberries are one of the rare fruits that you don't want to oversweeten, because they tend to get sweeter as they freeze.

If you want to strain out the skins, do so now. Press the blueberry mixture though a colander or sieve using a wooden spoon, a rubber spatula, or your fist (blueberries stain skin, so those choosing the third route might want to wear gloves). Or don't. Swirl in the buttermilk, minimally if you want a marbled effect, maximally if you want the flavors to coalesce.

Pour the mixture into your ice pop molds, leaving a little bit of room at the top for the mixture to expand. Insert sticks and freeze until solid, 4 to 5 hours. Unmold and transfer to plastic bags for storage or serve at once.

blueberry & cardamom

There's this really weird thing about working with blueberries. Once you purée them, they start to oxidize: whatever surface is exposed to the air turns brown, and the mass jells into a big block of what looks like purple-brown tofu. Thankfully, this process does not seem to have an effect on the pops' flavor, but it's freaky. Keep your composure and reserve judgment until you taste this pop, one of the first we ever made. Cardamom gives it a cinnamon-and-ginger-like flavor: earthy, sexy, and sweet. MAKES 10 POPS

8 to 10 green cardamom pods
1 cup (8 fl oz) simple syrup (page 7)
1¹/₃ pounds (4¹/₂ cups) blueberries
2 tablespoons (1 fl oz) freshly squeezed lemon juice

Spread the cardamom pods on a flat surface and bang away at them with a wooden mallet, or any hard, blunt object. Once they crack open you will see fuzzy little black seeds inside.

Sweep all of the crushed pods and their debris into a small saucepan and add the simple syrup. Cover and bring to a simmer over medium-high heat, then turn off the heat and let rest while the spices steep for 10 to 15 minutes. Be careful not to simmer the mixture for too long, because the simple syrup evaporates quickly, reducing the amount of liquid remaining. You want 3/4 cup (6 fl oz) to work with. Let cool.

Pick out any stems or leaves from the blueberries, then purée them in a food processor. You should have about 2¹/₄ cups (18 fl oz) of purée.

Strain the crushed cardamom pods out of the simple syrup and discard the cardamom. Transfer the puréed blueberries to a bowl or measuring pitcher with a pouring spout, add the simple syrup and lemon juice, and stir well to combine. Taste; the mixture should be sweet but not overly so, because blueberries' sweetness tends to carry over into freezing quite well. The cardamom flavor should be present but not overpowering. Adjust to taste.

If you wish, now is the time to strain out the skins by pressing the gloppy blueberry morass though a colander or sieve using a wooden spoon, a rubber spatula, or your fist (blueberries stain skin, so those choosing the third route might want to wear gloves). If you're lazy, you don't have to do this, but we really recommend it in this particular pop, because the flavor is so refined that it's worth the extra work.

Pour the mixture into your ice pop molds, leaving a little bit of room at the top for the mixture to expand. Insert sticks and freeze until solid, 4 to 5 hours. Unmold and transfer to plastic bags for storage or serve at once.

blueberry moonshine

Ideally, this pop would be savored on a front porch somewhere in North Carolina, surrounded by fireflies and the chirp of crickets and accompanied by the languorous strains of a bluegrass Dobro, but it's pretty good even in a crappy apartment in the city. In a bizarre postmodern reversal, these days you can buy moonshine in the most discerning liquor stores (try the Catdaddy brand).

As when making any type of boozy pop, pour lightly, because alcohol—and moonshine in particular, it seems—makes the pops really fragile. MAKES 10 POPS

1 pound 6 ounces (4³/4 cups) blueberries
²/3 cup (5 fl oz) simple syrup (page 7)
2 tablespoons (1 fl oz) freshly squeezed lemon juice
¹/3 cup (3 fl oz) moonshine

Pick out any stems or leaves from the blueberries and purée them in a food processor. You should have about 2¹/4 cups (18 fl oz) of purée.

Combine the puréed blueberries, simple syrup, and lemon juice in a bowl or measuring pitcher with a pouring spout. Taste; the precise amount of simple syrup and lemon juice needed will depend on how sweet the berries were to begin with. Be aware that blueberries are one of the rare fruits that you don't want to oversweeten because they tend to get sweeter as they freeze. Stir in the moonshine.

If you wish, now is the time to strain out the skins by pressing the gloppy blueberry mixture though a colander or sieve using a wooden spoon, a rubber spatula, or your fist (blueberries stain skin, so those choosing the third route might want to wear gloves). Or don't, and leave them in.

Pour the mixture into your ice pop molds, leaving a little bit of room at the top for the mixture to expand. Insert sticks and freeze until solid, 4 to 5 hours. Unmold and transfer to plastic bags for storage or serve at once.

straight-up raspberry

This recipe is simple, straightforward, and insouciantly delicious. Anyone between the ages of 2 and 102 is guaranteed to love it.   MAKES 10 POPS

1 pound (4 cups) raspberries
1 cup plus 2 tablespoons (9 fl oz) simple syrup (page 7)

Purée the raspberries in a food processor or just smash them with a potato masher, then transfer them to a bowl or measuring pitcher with a pouring spout. Add the simple syrup. Stir well and taste; the mixture should excite you! Adjust to taste until it does.

Pour the mixture into your ice pop molds, leaving a little bit of room at the top for the mixture to expand. Insert sticks and freeze until solid, 4 to 5 hours. Unmold and transfer to plastic bags for storage or serve at once.

raspberries & basil

Much to our surprise, this pop blew the roof off of 2010. We thought people might be put off by the bizarre-sounding combination, but it didn't seem to faze anyone. Everyone—even children—loved this pop. The basil is sneaky good, and the raspberries pack a serious punch. We usually leave in the raspberry seeds, which lend the pop a nice crunch, but straining them out makes for a refined texture and lets the bold flavor really sing. You'll need 1¹/₄ pounds (5 cups) raspberries if you're going to strain out the seeds. **MAKES 10 POPS**

1¹/₃ cups (11 fl oz) simple syrup (page 7)
Leaves from three 6-inch sprigs fresh basil
1 pound (4 cups) raspberries

Combine the simple syrup and basil leaves in a small saucepan. Heat over medium heat, covered, until simmering cheerily, then turn off the heat and let rest while the leaves steep. Be careful not to simmer the mixture for too long, because the simple syrup evaporates quickly, reducing the amount of liquid remaining. You want 1 cup plus 2 tablespoons (9 fl oz) to work with. Let cool.

Purée the raspberries in a food processor or mash them with a potato masher.

Strain out the basil, squeeze it over the simple syrup to extract as much liquid as possible, and discard. Combine the basil-scented simple syrup with the puréed raspberries in a bowl or measuring pitcher with a pouring spout. Doesn't it smell a bit like marijuana? Yes, it does! The mixture should taste sweet, be brightly acidic, and have a delicious, lingering basil-y aroma. This pop is definitely more than the sum of its parts.

Pour the mixture into your ice pop molds, leaving a little bit of room at the top for the mixture to expand. Insert sticks and freeze until solid, 4 to 5 hours. Unmold and transfer to plastic bags for storage or serve at once.

raspberries & cream

This is the prettiest pop we make. We like to dribble a little bit of extra cream down one side of the mold (don't overdo it—a teaspoon is plenty). The cream will drip down and collect at the bottom of the mold, and when you pour in the raspberry mixture, the swirly effect is gorgeous. When Martha Stewart had one of these she said it was the best pop she'd ever tasted. The moment is immortalized in a photograph that we've proudly hung in our Chelsea shop.   MAKES 10 POPS

1 pound (4 cups) raspberries
$^2/_3$ cup (5 fl oz) simple syrup (page 7)
$^1/_2$ cup (4 fl oz) heavy cream

Purée the raspberries in a food processor or smash with a potato masher. Transfer them to a bowl or measuring pitcher with a pouring spout and add the simple syrup. Stir well and taste; significant seasonal variation in raspberries means the sweetness of your mixture may need tweaking. Add the cream and stir very, very minimally. The swirl effect in the finished pop is an aesthetic (and gustatory) effect really worth trying to achieve, and the act of pouring the cream into the molds will do a lot to homogenize the mixture, so don't overmix it.

Pour the mixture into your ice pop molds, leaving a little bit of room at the top for the mixture to expand. Insert sticks and freeze until solid, 4 to 5 hours. Unmold and transfer to plastic bags for storage or serve at once.

raspberry jam & yogurt

No fruit in the house? Don't despair. This is a great pantry pop you can make in no time; we love its robustly chewy, taffylike texture. The proportions will really depend on how sweet your jam is, so don't blindly adhere to the quantities below. We like to use organic vanilla yogurt, which usually comes sweetened, so if you're using plain yogurt, adjust the recipe accordingly. You can use cream instead of yogurt for an incredibly rich pop that tastes almost like ice cream. If you really want to go the distance, make your own jam. You'll find nonintimidating tips for making great jam in any of Darina Allen's books or Kelly Geary's *Tart and Sweet*.   MAKES 10 POPS

1 1/2 cups (12 fl oz) raspberry jam, purchased or homemade
1 cup plus 2 tablespoons (9 fl oz) water
1/2 cup (4 fl oz) organic vanilla yogurt

In a bowl or measuring pitcher with a pouring spout, combine the jam and water until they are well mixed. Add the yogurt and taste for sweetness, raspberry flavor, and the subtle tang of balanced acidity. Re-jig if necessary.

Pour the mixture into your ice pop molds, leaving a little bit of room at the top for the mixture to expand. Insert sticks and freeze until solid, 4 to 5 hours. Unmold and transfer to plastic bags for storage or serve at once.

sour cherry & almond

A little-known fact about stone fruits such as cherries, apricots, and peaches is that within their hard pit lies a tiny inner pit that can be toxic when consumed raw but tastes like almonds once roasted (they're a popular snack in the 'stans of Central Asia). This got us thinking about pairing almonds with stone fruits, and so this pop was born.

   If you don't want to go through the folderol of pitting cherries but like this idea, try making a strawberry-almond pop. Use 2¼ cups (18 fl oz) puréed strawberries, ¾ cup plus 2 tablespoons (7 fl oz) simple syrup, and ½ to 1 tablespoon almond extract.   MAKES 10 POPS

1 pound 6 ounces (scant 5 cups) fresh sour cherries, or 2 pounds 2 ounces
(7½ cups) canned sour cherries with their liquid

⅔ cup (5 ounces) organic cane sugar

½ to 1 tablespoon almond extract

If you are using fresh fruit, remove any stems. Pit them using a cherry pitter or a paring knife.

   Pour about ½ inch of water into a shallow, heavy, nonreactive saucepan and add the cherries. If you are using canned cherries, dump them, liquid and all, into the saucepan. Cook over low heat, stirring frequently to make sure the cherries don't burn, until soft and crimson and the cherries have released a lot of juice, about 15 minutes. Drain the cherries, reserving the cherries and their juice separately.

   Combine ⅔ cup (5 fl oz) of the strained cherry juice with the sugar in a saucepan, saving the rest of the cherry juice for another use. Cook over medium heat, stirring occasionally, until the sugar dissolves, then remove from the heat.

   While the liquid heats, purée the cherries in a food processor. If they are not fairly finely puréed, the pop mixture will be hard to pour and the chunks will turn icy.

continued

In a bowl or measuring pitcher with a pouring spout, combine 2 cups plus 2 tablespoons (17 fl oz) puréed cherries with 1 cup (8 fl oz) of the cherry simple syrup. Taste; adjust if the mixture isn't sweet enough. Add the almond extract bit by bit until you can taste the amaretto-like flavor coming through boldly and clearly. But don't overdo it! A little goes a long way.

Pour the mixture into your ice pop molds, leaving a little bit of room at the top for the mixture to expand. Insert sticks and freeze until solid, 4 to 5 hours. Unmold and transfer to plastic bags for storage or serve at once.

blackberry & rose

This is a delicate, ladylike, almost Victorian-tasting pop. We like the textural finesse that results from straining out the seeds, but straining it is not absolutely necessary. If you aren't going to strain the seeds, use only 1½ pounds (5 cups) blackberries. The subtle, elegant flavor of rose can also be used to domesticate peaches, plums, quince, or pears. **MAKES 10 POPS**

1 pound 11 ounces (6½ cups) blackberries
3/4 cup plus 2 tablespoons (7 fl oz) simple syrup (page 7)
1 tablespoon freshly squeezed lemon juice
1 tablespoon rosewater

Purée the blackberries in a food processor or mash them well using a potato masher. You should have about 2 cups plus 2 tablespoons (17 fl oz) of purée.

Transfer the puréed blackberries to a bowl or measuring pitcher with a pouring spout and stir in the simple syrup and lemon juice. Add the rosewater bit by bit, stopping when you get to "lovely floral essence" but before "potpourri."

Strain the mixture through a colander or sieve (blackberries stain skin, so you might want to wear gloves if you're using your hands to push them through).

Pour the mixture into your ice pop molds, leaving a little bit of room at the top for the mixture to expand. Insert sticks and freeze until solid, 4 to 5 hours. Unmold and transfer to plastic bags for storage or serve at once.

blackberry, yogurt & honey

For a while there was a beehive on the roof of Nathalie's New York apartment. The bees were prodigious producers of a honey that tasted wonderfully floral, despite the high levels of mercury, pollution, and who knows what else was undoubtedly lingering in the air around her dirty corner of the Lower East Side. This recipe was originally published in *Bon Appétit* in August 2010 and tweaked for inclusion here. If not straining out the seeds, you'll only need 15 ounces (3 cups) blackberries.   MAKES 10 POPS

1 pound (3¹/₂ cups) blackberries

²/₃ cup (5 fl oz) simple syrup (page 7)

¹/₂ cup (4 fl oz) organic plain nonfat yogurt

2 to 4 tablespoons (1 to 2 fl oz) honey

2 tablespoons (1 fl oz) freshly squeezed lemon juice

Purée the blackberries in a food processor until smooth. Add the simple syrup, yogurt, honey, and lemon juice. Whisk to blend. Can you taste the honey? If not, add a bit more.

Strain this mixture into a bowl or measuring pitcher with a pouring spout, extracting as much purée as possible. Discard the seeds.

Pour the mixture into your ice pop molds, leaving a little bit of room at the top for the mixture to expand. Insert sticks and freeze until solid, 4 to 5 hours. Unmold and transfer to plastic bags for storage or serve at once.

blackberry & lemon verbena

Consider yourself warned that the mixture for this pop tastes so dang good that you might want to make a little extra, because you're apt to find yourself licking the bowl clean before you've even started pouring the pops. Verbena is a great aid to low-acidity fruits such as blueberries, grapes, melons, and cucumbers, but we think blackberries pair with it best.   MAKES 10 POPS

Just over 1 cup (8 fl oz) simple syrup (page 7)
$^1/_2$ ounce (2$^1/_2$ tablespoons) fresh or dried lemon verbena leaves, or 3 to 4 lemon verbena tea bags
Just under 2 pounds (scant 7 cups) blackberries

Pour the simple syrup into a small saucepan. Cover and bring to a simmer over medium heat. Once the liquid starts to bubble, uncover and drop in the lemon verbena leaves or tea bags, then recover the saucepan. Turn off the heat and let rest while the lemon verbena steeps. Be careful not to simmer the mixture for too long, because the simple syrup evaporates quickly, reducing the amount of liquid remaining. You want $^3/_4$ cup plus 2 tablespoons (7 fl oz) to work with. Let cool.

Purée the blackberries in a food processor or mash them well with a potato masher. You should have about 2$^1/_3$ cups (19 fl oz) of purée.

Strain out the lemon verbena and squeeze it over the simple syrup to extract as much liquid as possible.

Do not discard. Transfer the puréed blackberries to a bowl or measuring pitcher with a pouring spout and add the lemon verbena simple syrup. It should taste lemony and bright and, if you're using the same strain of lemon verbena as we do, inexplicably a bit like cookie dough. Now, strain the mixture through a colander or sieve (blackberries stain skin, so you might want to wear gloves if you're using your hands to push them through).

Pour the mixture into your ice pop molds, leaving a little bit of room at the top for the mixture to expand. Insert sticks and freeze until solid, 4 to 5 hours. Unmold and transfer to plastic bags for storage or serve at once.

DISPATCH FROM THE FIELD

We've learned a *lot* as we have built our pop-making business.

How to buy a van off Craigslist. How to deal with the fact that the insurance costs more than what we paid for the van. How to extract more credit from a bank so tightly wound that we've gotten bigger tips as waiters than the credit they've extended to us. Not kidding.

Navigating the vagaries of various city departments: Revenue, Special Events, the Division of Milk Control and Dairy Services, Licensing and Permits, Ag & Markets, and Consumer Affairs, to name a few. Finding out—quickly—where to go when our supplier is out of dry ice and we've got a freezer full of melting pops.

Designing ingredient labels that the Department of Health will approve. Stamping pop sticks by hand, on both sides, one thousand at a time. Realizing that food-safe ink wasn't used. Realizing that they'll work just fine as business cards.

And then there's our technique. What are the most efficient, wasteless ways to hull strawberries or wash rhubarb or measure out simple syrup? What's the ideal sugar level in a given pop mixture, and how can we constantly achieve it when our ingredients change from week to week? What are the cleanest, most sensible ways to pour pops, unmold them, and wrap them?

What is the best proportion of gin to tonic after a long day's work? Might it be 100 percent gin, or does that just seem like the right solution when the bottle of tonic is empty and we're too tired to walk downstairs to the bodega?

Will it cost more to hire people to work the stands or open fewer stands and manage them ourselves? And how can we make the bloody rain stop? How do we keep up with the endless ribbons of receipts for antibacterial wipes, pH test strips, food prep bucket lids, chalkboard paint, 7-ounce cups, black mint, boxes of pop sticks, organic lemons, a couple hundred pounds of sugar, Department of Health permits, Department of Ag & Market permits, and dry ice, to name about a quarter of the things we spent money on this week?

How can we stay sane in the face of all these questions?

Now *that* is a good question.

midsummer

people's pops

APRICOTS

apricot & lavender | 56

apricot & orange blossom | 57

apricot & salted caramel | 58

PEACHES

peach & jalapeño | 60

roasted yellow peach | 62

peach & bourbon | 63

NECTARINES

nectarine, honey & chamomile | 64

roasted nectarine & basil | 65

PLUMS

roasted red plum | 67

plum, yogurt & tarragon | 68

damson plum with shiso | 70

PLOTTING THE FRUIT SEASON along a mathematical curve looks kind of like this. For most of the year, there's zilch—and then, all of a sudden, *le déluge.*

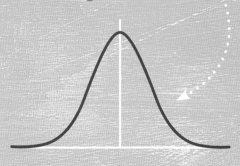

If we had any kind of foresight (we don't), this is when we'd buy fruit and freeze it ourselves. Although we may not be organized enough to freeze fruit ahead of time, when we transform it into ice pops, we are, in a sense, following in the footsteps of an age-old tradition: saving excess bounty with an eye to the future. In the same way that cheese is "milk's leap toward immortality" (according to Clifton Fadiman), ice pops are essentially a way of preserving an overabundance of food, of adding value to fruit that might otherwise rot on the tree or in the basket.

If you are lucky enough to have access to loads of fresh fruit and want to preserve it for the winter, the best way to do so is to start by washing and prepping it—hull the strawberries, stone the plums, pit the cherries. When the fruit has totally dried (this is important), spread it out on trays in one layer and freeze it. Once it's frozen, fill airtight resealable plastic bags with the fruit. The more quickly the fruit freezes, the better the end result.

Most of the recipes in this chapter call for stewing or roasting the fruit. This serves three purposes: first, it makes the pits easier to remove; second, it softens the flesh of fruits that may not be entirely ripe; and, third, roasting adds a gorgeous depth of flavor. However, this step is not entirely necessary. If you've got really ripe or overripe fruit, you can skip it. Also, using raw fruit gives the pop a different, fresh, crunchy taste and texture that you might enjoy for a change. As long as you're using great fruit, it's hard to go wrong.

apricots

Apricots are bafflingly underrated. We often have to talk people into choosing apricot pops over more obvious options such as strawberry or raspberry. Those in the know, however, realize that they make tremendous pops, redolent with the flavors of peach and melon, and apricots can be paired with some really sophisticated flavors. Their flesh melts into a soft, velvety texture, and their natural acidity requires no extra boost. You can use apricots raw, especially if they're very ripe, but we prefer to stew them on the stove.

Apricots should be fully yellow-orange over their entire surface, feel slightly soft when pressed, and smell delicious. Don't choose any that feel hard or have no aroma.

In addition to our suggestions in this chapter, apricots also pair beautifully with almonds, cream, star anise, or vanilla.

peaches

Few fruits epitomize the height of summer better than a super-ripe, pour-down-your-arms-to-your-elbows-juicy peach. If you can, seek out white peaches, which are slightly less common but have a particularly gorgeous flavor. Even the ripest peaches will benefit from a touch of freshly squeezed lemon juice.

When choosing peaches, look for fruits that are brightly colored and fragrant and feel firm with a slight give. Avoid greenish peaches, which are too young; wrinkled peaches, which are too old; and fruit with soft spots or blemishes. Although peaches will not ripen after picking, they will soften and become juicier if left at room temperature or in a paper bag with an apple or a banana.

As with the other stone fruits, we recommend roasting peaches before puréeing them unless you've managed to score extremely ripe fruit. We happen to like the textural interest peach skin offers (and that's where most of the vitamins are), so we rarely peel peaches. If, however, you want a really uniform texture with no peels, use a sharp knife to make an X

cream, ginger, rum, pomegranate molasses, vanilla, or whatever! As long as the peaches are ripe and sweet, you really can't go wrong.

nectarines

The world is filled with mediocre nectarines. They nestle insidiously in the brown paper lunch bags of children and near the checkout lines of corporate cafeterias all over the country. Excellent tree-ripened nectarines are to these crappy ersatz nects what surround sound is to a transistor radio. Seek out the white or yellow varieties in season at your farmers' market and make these amazingly soft-textured, heart-warming pops.

Although some people erroneously believe that nectarines are a cross between peaches and plums, they are actually just peaches with a recessive bald gene that makes them fuzzless. Whatever. We're equal opportunity when it comes to stone fruit.

As with peaches, you can roast or stew nectarines or leave them raw. Each method will result in a different texture and flavor. Unless the fruit is superlatively ripe, roasting it is our preference. A bit of freshly squeezed lemon juice boosts the flavor, too.

in the base of the fruit, plunge the peach into boiling water for 20 seconds, and then, with a slotted spoon, transfer it to a bowl of ice water. The skin should peel away from the flesh pretty easily.

Once you've exhausted the peach recipes in this chapter, think about pairing peaches with, well, pretty much anything. Peaches are friendlier than almost any fruit other than rhubarb. Think about peaches with basil, bitters, tarragon (amazing),

plums

Plums freeze beautifully, produce copious amounts of juice when cooked, and have a lovely tart flavor that pairs with a gamut of flavors, from bitters to celery to rosewater to rum. They also come in varieties that manifest all colors of the rainbow: plain red, purple pluots and damsons, lime-colored greengages, yellow mirabelles and shiros, and nearly black plums. You can use any variety of plum in the recipes in this chapter, but the quantities required may differ a bit as a result. If you're a real dork (like us), create a multicolored plum pop by making various mixtures with differently colored plums and layering them in the molds, waiting for each layer to freeze before you pour in the next one.

Make sure you manage to fully pit the plums before puréeing your mixture. Not only do you risk breaking your processor blade on a hard pit, but you also risk breaking a tooth if any loose bits make it into the pop. We prefer roasting or stewing the plums to leaving them raw (particularly because of the delicious syrup this creates, which we can then turn into shave ice), but raw plums, which produce an icier, more brightly flavored pop, taste fine also. The use of freshly squeezed lemon juice to brighten the acidity is optional; it depends on the level of natural acidity the plums bring to the table.

apricot & lavender

This is a pop that we were delighted to learn tastes as good as it sounds. It's the quintessence of summer . . . on a stick. We usually buy lavender at the farmers' market, but you can buy bottled lavender buds in the spice aisle of many grocery stores. Lavender also makes a good match with cantaloupe, rhubarb, blueberries, and figs. But don't overdo it, or it won't go with anything! | MAKES 10 POPS

1 pound 10 ounces apricots (9 to 10), halved and pitted
Just over 1 cup (8 fl oz) simple syrup (page 7)
1 tablespoon dried lavender buds, or 6 sprigs fresh or dried lavender, including stems

Pour about ¹/₂ inch of water into a heavy, nonreactive saucepan and add the apricots. Stew the apricots over medium heat until the skins and flesh have softened, 20 to 25 minutes. (If they're very ripe, feel free to use them raw.)

Combine the simple syrup and lavender in a small saucepan. Cover and bring to a simmer over medium-high heat for 5 to 10 minutes. Turn off the heat and let rest while the lavender steeps. Be careful not to simmer the mixture for too long, because the simple syrup evaporates quickly, reducing the amount of liquid. You want ³/₄ cup plus 2 tablespoons (7 fl oz) to work with. Let cool.

Whiz the apricots, skins and all, in a food processor, though feel free to leave the purée

somewhat chunky. You should have about 2¹/₄ cups (18 fl oz) of purée.

Strain the lavender out of the simple syrup and discard the flowers. Transfer the puréed apricots to a bowl or measuring pitcher with a pouring spout and add the lavender simple syrup. Stir and taste; the lavender should come through without the mixture tasting like soap. Adjust if necessary.

Pour the mixture into your ice pop molds, leaving a little bit of room at the top for the mixture to expand. Insert sticks and freeze until solid, 4 to 5 hours. Unmold and transfer to plastic bags for storage or serve at once.

apricot & orange blossom

Apricots are popular in North Africa, where orange blossom water is also commonly used. None of us has spent that much time in North Africa, but this seemed like a natural pairing. You can buy orange blossom water at an international grocery, at many liquor stores, or online. Cortas, which is very concentrated, is a good brand. If you use another brand, you might need to add more. Orange blossom water also pairs well with strawberries, pears, and peaches. | MAKES 10 POPS

1^1/$_2$ pounds apricots (8 to 9), halved and pitted

3/4 cup (6 fl oz) simple syrup (page 7), or more if needed

1 to 2 teaspoons orange blossom water

Pour about ^{1}/$_2$ inch of water into a heavy, nonreactive saucepan and add the apricots. Stew the apricots over medium heat until the skins and flesh have softened, 20 to 25 minutes. (If they're very ripe, feel free to use them raw.)

Whiz the apricots, skins and all, in a food processor, though feel free to leave the purée somewhat chunky. You should have about 2^1/$_4$ cups (18 fl oz) of purée.

Transfer the puréed apricots to a bowl or measuring pitcher with a pouring spout and add the simple syrup. Stir until the mixture is well incorporated. Taste; the mixture should be sweet and slightly tart. Add the orange blossom water bit by bit—it is very strong stuff. Stop when the mixture is fragrant but before it smells like detergent.

Pour the mixture into your ice pop molds, leaving a little bit of room at the top for the mixture to expand. Insert sticks and freeze until solid, 4 to 5 hours. Unmold and transfer to plastic bags for storage or serve at once.

apricot & salted caramel

Joel came up with this pop. It sounds bizarre, but it has a complex, swoony flavor and a killer texture. Trust us and make it. | MAKES 10 POPS

1 pound 6 ounces apricots (7 to 8), halved and pitted
$^1/_2$ cup (4 fl oz) salted caramel (see opposite)
$^3/_4$ cup (6 fl oz) simple syrup (page 7)

Pour about $^1/_2$ inch of water into a heavy, nonreactive saucepan and add the apricots. Stew the apricots over medium heat until the skins and flesh have softened, 20 to 25 minutes. (If they're very ripe, feel free to use them raw.)

As the apricots cook, make the caramel (see opposite). The caramel can also be made ahead of time, if you like.

Whiz the apricots, skins and all, in a food processor, though feel free to leave the purée somewhat chunky. You should have about 1$^3/_4$ cups plus 2 tablespoons (15 fl oz) of purée.

Transfer the puréed apricots to a bowl or measuring pitcher with a pouring spout and add the simple syrup. Add the caramel and stir until the mixture is well incorporated (resist the temptation to pour all of the caramel from the recipe opposite into the mixture or it will overpower the pop. Eat the last 2 tablespoons yourself!). Taste; the mixture should be complex and interesting, with the flavor of the caramel coming through without overwhelming the apricots.

Pour the mixture into your ice pop molds, leaving a little bit of room at the top for the mixture to expand. Insert sticks and freeze until solid, 4 to 5 hours. Unmold and transfer to plastic bags for storage or serve at once.

salted caramel

The extra ounce that this makes is for you to lick off the spoon. It's that good! | MAKES ²/₃ CUP (5 FL OZ)

¹/₂ cup (4 oz) organic cane sugar

2 tablespoons (1 oz) unsalted butter

¹/₄ cup (2 fl oz) heavy cream

Kosher salt

Place the sugar in a heavy saucepan and melt it over high heat until it darkens to a light amber color. You can let it get a little darker, but the caramel turns bitter by the time it becomes mahogany. Add the butter and stir. Once the butter melts, take the pan off the heat and add the cream *very* slowly. Be careful not to burn yourself. Add salt to taste, about ¹/₄ teaspoon. The mixture will be liquid when warm, but if cold, just put it in the microwave for a few seconds and it will soften again.

peach & jalapeño

In Mexico there is a long tradition of making ice pops, known as *paletas*, with tropical fruits such as mango, coconut, tamarind, papaya, avocado, and citrus. We love these, but because most of them are made with fruits that don't grow in our area, we've rarely attempted to replicate their flavors. This combination, however, is one locally sourced way to pay homage to that delicious tradition. | MAKES 10 POPS

1 pound 6 ounces peaches (about 4 to 5 tennis ball–sized), halved

1¹/₄ cups (10 fl oz) simple syrup (page 7)

1 jalapeño pepper, thinly sliced

2 tablespoons (1 fl oz) freshly squeezed lemon juice

Preheat the oven to 350°F. Place the peaches cut side down on a cookie sheet. Bake until the skins and flesh have softened, about 20 minutes. Remove from the oven and let cool.

Combine the simple syrup and jalapeño in a small saucepan. Cover and bring to a simmer over medium heat. After 5 to 10 minutes, turn off the heat and let rest while the pepper steeps. Be careful not to simmer the mixture for too long, because the simple syrup evaporates quickly, reducing the amount of liquid remaining. You want 1 cup (8 fl oz) to work with. Let cool.

Once the peaches are cool enough to touch, remove and discard the pits and whiz the peaches, skins and all, in a food processor, though feel free to leave the purée somewhat chunky. You should have about 2 cups (16 fl oz) of purée.

Strain the jalapeño out of the simple syrup and discard the jalapeño. Transfer the puréed peaches to a bowl or measuring pitcher with a pouring spout and add the jalapeño simple syrup and the lemon juice. Stir until the mixture is well incorporated. Dip a spoon in; the peach should taste sweet, but accented by a piquant bite from the jalapeño.

Pour the mixture into your ice pop molds, leaving a little bit of room at the top for the mixture to expand. Insert sticks and freeze until solid, 4 to 5 hours. Unmold and transfer to plastic bags for storage or serve at once.

roasted yellow peach

This method of preparing a peach pop showcases the fruit's simple, ambrosial beauty. Needless to say, using great fruit makes a big difference. You can certainly use raw fruit, especially if it is very ripe (if you do, use only 1 pound 2 ounces), but we like to roast the peaches for an additional layer of flavor. You might also add 1 teaspoon vanilla extract for a lovely warm touch. | MAKES 10 POPS

1 pound 5 ounces peaches (4 to 5 tennis ball–sized), halved
1 cup (8 fl oz) simple syrup (page 7)
2 tablespoons (1 fl oz) freshly squeezed lemon juice

Preheat the oven to 350°F. Place the peaches cut side down on a cookie sheet. Bake until the skins and flesh have softened, about 20 minutes. Remove from the oven and let cool.

Once the peaches are cool enough to touch, remove and discard the pits and whiz the peaches, skins and all, in a food processor, though feel free to leave the purée somewhat chunky. You should have about 2 cups (16 fl oz) of purée.

Transfer the puréed peaches to a bowl or measuring pitcher with a pouring spout and add the simple syrup and lemon juice. Stir until the mixture is well incorporated. Taste; the mixture should be sweet and ambrosially peachy.

Pour the mixture into your ice pop molds, leaving a little bit of room at the top for the mixture to expand. Insert sticks and freeze until solid, 4 to 5 hours. Unmold and transfer to plastic bags for storage or serve at once.

peach & bourbon

Here we pay tribute to the American South with Georgia peaches and Kentucky bourbon. Slurp. Yum. The booze gives this pop a really wonderful melty texture. If you have very ripe fruit and choose not to roast it, you'll need just 1 pound 2 ounces peaches. Be careful not to use too much booze or the pop won't freeze completely. | MAKES 10 POPS

$1^1/_4$ pounds peaches (4 to 5 tennis ball–sized), halved
$3/_4$ cup (6 fl oz) simple syrup (page 7)
$1/_3$ cup (3 fl oz) bourbon or whiskey, plus extra for drinking
2 tablespoons (1 fl oz) freshly squeezed lemon juice

Preheat the oven to 350°F. Place the peaches cut side down on a cookie sheet. Bake until the skins and flesh have softened, about 20 minutes. Remove from the oven and let cool.

Once the peaches are cool enough to touch, remove and discard the pits and whiz the peaches, skins and all, in a food processor, though feel free to leave the purée somewhat chunky. You should have about 2 cups (16 fl oz) of purée.

Transfer the puréed peaches to a bowl or measuring pitcher with a pouring spout and add the simple syrup, bourbon, and lemon juice. Stir until the mixture is well incorporated, and have a glass of bourbon on ice to celebrate your hard work.

Pour the mixture into your ice pop molds, leaving a little bit of room at the top for the mixture to expand. Insert sticks and freeze until solid, 4 to 5 hours. Unmold and transfer to plastic bags for storage or serve at once.

nectarine, honey & chamomile

After the first day that People's Pops opened, David and Joel had to make the pops without Nathalie for the rest of the summer. Neither of them had a cooking background: David had worked for a television network, and Joel was a prop stylist for photo shoots. But when they came up with this pop, it more than proved that they could be trusted in the kitchen. Subtle, haunting, and ephemeral, this is the epitome of the perfect mid-summer pop.

If you can't put your hands on fresh chamomile flowers (available in season at the farmers' market), you can use one chamomile tea bag instead. Use extremely ripe nectarines for this recipe. Otherwise, add one extra nectarine to the quantity and roast them, following the directions for the Roasted Nectarine & Basil pops (see opposite). | MAKES 10 POPS

2 pounds extremely ripe nectarines (about 7), halved and pitted

1/4 cup (2 fl oz) honey, or more if needed

2 tablespoons (1 fl oz) freshly squeezed lemon juice

3 fresh chamomile flowers, finely minced

Pinch of kosher salt

Purée two-thirds of the nectarines, skin and all, until the mixture is almost smooth. Transfer to a bowl or measuring pitcher with a pouring spout and stir in the honey, lemon juice, chamomile flowers, and salt. Coarsely chop the remaining one-third of the nectarines and stir into the purée. If you can't taste the honey, add more. Remember to make these pops a tad sweeter than you think they need to be; they lose a little sweetness after freezing.

Pour the mixture into your ice pop molds, leaving a little bit of room at the top for the mixture to expand. Insert sticks and freeze until solid, 4 to 5 hours. Unmold and transfer to plastic bags for storage or serve at once.

roasted nectarine & basil

This pop is pure July: fleshy, full-throated nectarines, leafy basil, hot sun, cold beer. Leave the nectarines raw if you wish (if you do, use just four), or roast them, as described below. Peach-basil is a terrific alternative to this recipe, and so are nectarine-tarragon and peach-tarragon. Use the same proportions as given for these variations. | MAKES 10 POPS

1¼ pounds nectarines (4 to 5), halved
1 cup plus 2 tablespoons (9 fl oz) simple syrup (page 7)
3 leafy sprigs basil, each about 6 inches long
2 tablespoons (1 fl oz) freshly squeezed lemon juice

Preheat the oven to 350°F. Place the nectarines cut side down on a cookie sheet, then roast until the skins and flesh have softened, about 20 minutes. Remove from the oven and let cool.

While the nectarines cook, combine the simple syrup and basil in a small saucepan. Cover and bring to a simmer over medium heat. Turn off the heat and let rest while the leaves steep. Be careful not to simmer the mixture for too long, because the simple syrup evaporates quickly, reducing the amount of liquid remaining. You want 1 cup (8 fl oz) to work with. Let cool.

Once the nectarines are cool enough to touch, remove and discard the pits and whiz the nectarines, skins and all, in a food processor, though feel free to leave the purée somewhat chunky. You should have about 2 cups (16 fl oz) of purée.

Strain out the basil, squeeze it over the simple syrup to extract as much liquid as possible, and discard. Transfer the puréed nectarines to a bowl or measuring pitcher with a pouring spout and add the basil simple syrup and the lemon juice. Stir until the mixture is well incorporated and taste. The flavor of the basil should be solidly present against a sweet and wholesome nectarine backdrop.

Pour the mixture into your ice pop molds, leaving a little bit of room at the top for the mixture to expand. Insert sticks and freeze until solid, 4 to 5 hours. Unmold and transfer to plastic bags for storage or serve at once.

roasted red plum

This pop suits any time of year. If you feel like it, doll up the simple syrup with vanilla, star anise, cardamom, or cinnamon (wintry!), or just leave the plum plain and simple (summery). If flavoring the simple syrup, start with $1^1/4$ cups (10 fl oz), because it will reduce upon cooking. For direction on achieving the natty striped pop featured opposite, consult page 55. Yellow plums, Nath's favorite, make killer pops, too. We like to roast or stew the plums and have instructed you to do so below, but you can leave them raw. If you do, start with only 1 pound of plums. | MAKES 10 POPS

$1^1/4$ pounds plums (about 12 small or 5 large), halved

1 cup (8 fl oz) simple syrup (page 7)

Preheat the oven to 350°F. Place the plums cut side down on a cookie sheet, then roast until the skins and flesh have significantly softened, 20 to 40 minutes. Remove from the oven and let cool.

Once the plums are cool enough to touch, remove and discard the pits and whiz the plums, skins and all, in a food processor, though feel free to leave the purée somewhat chunky. You should have about $2^1/8$ cups (17 fl oz) of purée.

Transfer the puréed plums to a bowl or measuring pitcher with a pouring spout and add the simple syrup. Stir until the mixture is well incorporated and taste. The mixture should be sweet yet slightly tart.

Pour the mixture into your ice pop molds, leaving a little bit of room at the top for the mixture to expand. Insert sticks and freeze until solid, 4 to 5 hours. Unmold and transfer to plastic bags for storage or serve at once.

plum, yogurt & tarragon

This definitely belongs on the list of the Top Ten Pops We've Ever Made. Three of the most versatile ingredients we use combine to make a genius pop that is definitely greater than the sum of its parts. If we ever have kids, we want them to turn out like this: complex, intelligent, gentle, mellow, and appealing. | MAKES 10 POPS

1 pound plums (8 to 9 small or 3 to 4 large), halved
1 cup (8 fl oz) simple syrup (page 7)
2 to 3 sprigs tarragon, or more as needed
2 tablespoons (1 fl oz) freshly squeezed lemon juice
1/2 cup (4 fl oz) organic vanilla yogurt

Preheat the oven to 350°F. Place the plums cut side down on a cookie sheet, then roast until the skins and flesh have significantly softened, 20 to 40 minutes. Remove from the oven and let cool.

While the plums cook, combine the simple syrup and tarragon (stems and all) in a small saucepan. Cover and bring to a simmer over medium heat. Simmer for 5 to 10 minutes, then turn off the heat and let rest while the tarragon steeps. Be careful not to heat the mixture for too long, because the simple syrup evaporates quickly, reducing the amount of liquid remaining. You want 3/4 cup plus 2 tablespoons (7 fl oz) to work with. Let cool. Can

you smell the tarragon? If not, discard the spent tarragon, add a few new springs of tarragon to the syrup, and repeat the simmering process.

Once the plums are cool enough to touch, remove and discard the pits and whiz the plums, skins and all, in a food processor, though feel free to leave the purée somewhat chunky. You should have about 1²/3 cups (13 fl oz) of purée.

Strain out the tarragon, squeeze it over the simple syrup to extract as much liquid as possible, and discard the tarragon. Transfer the puréed plums to a bowl or measuring pitcher with a pouring spout and add the tarragon simple syrup and lemon juice. Stir

until the mixture is well incorporated and taste. The mixture should be sweet, with a licorice-y warmth emanating from the tarragon. Swirl in the yogurt. We typically use yogurt that is somewhat sweet, so if yours isn't, make sure the mixture tastes quite sweet at this point, because the sweetness will dull upon freezing.

Pour the mixture into your ice pop molds, leaving a little bit of room at the top for the mixture to expand. Insert sticks and freeze until solid, 4 to 5 hours. Unmold and transfer to plastic bags for storage or serve at once.

damson plum with shiso

Shiso, an exotic Japanese relative of mint, crept into our consciousness by way of a delicious cocktail at a bar hidden behind the curtain of a Japanese restaurant in Manhattan's East Village called the Angel's Share. Although decidedly obscure, shiso has a ton of applications: use it in teas, desserts, cocktails, and other pops (with cucumber, rhubarb, blackberries, or watermelon, for instance). But if you can't find it, just use mint. Damsons are tiny wild plums that, incidentally, make fabulous jam, but this recipe will work with any plum relative. | MAKES 10 POPS

1¹/₄ pounds damson plums (12 to 15), halved and pitted
1¹/₃ cups (11 fl oz) simple syrup (page 7)
5 to 6 shiso leaves

Pour about ¹/₂ inch of water into a heavy, nonreactive saucepan and add the damsons. Cook over medium heat, stirring frequently, until the damsons have softened considerably, about 15 minutes.

While the damsons cook, combine the simple syrup and shiso leaves in a small saucepan. Cover and bring to a simmer over medium heat. Simmer for 5 to 10 minutes, then turn off the heat and let rest while the shiso steeps. Be careful not to simmer the mixture for too long, because the simple syrup evaporates quickly. You want 1 cup plus 2 tablespoons (9 fl oz) to work with. Let cool.

Once the damsons have cooked, whiz them, skins and all, in a food processor, though feel free to leave the purée somewhat chunky. You should have about 2 cups (16 fl oz) of purée.

Strain out the shiso, squeeze it over the simple syrup to extract as much liquid as possible, and discard the leaves. Transfer the puréed damsons to a bowl or measuring pitcher with a pouring spout and add the infused simple syrup. Stir until the mixture is well incorporated and taste. The mixture should be sweet, with a mysterious minty twinge. Adjust to taste.

Pour the mixture into your ice pop molds, leaving a little bit of room at the top for the mixture to expand. Insert sticks and freeze until solid, 4 to 5 hours. Unmold and transfer to plastic bags for storage or serve at once.

During the summer of 2010 we received an email from a professor at Brigham Young University who was taking a group of business students to New York and wanted to know if we'd be willing to spare a few minutes to talk about "the strategy behind People's Pops as an emerging brand."

Strategy? Is that what's happening while we're drinking wine on the sidewalk as we paint our sandwich boards?

We like being flattered, so we said yes, and after a long day in the kitchen Nathalie sped over to the shop, spattered with raspberry juice and the rotten pong of things left perennially undone. The nineteen students—clean-cut, well-mannered, inquisitive—had spent their morning at American Express and their afternoon at Johnson & Johnson. Nath told them the People's Pops story, how making pops for a one-day market with her prom date and his roommate unexpectedly turned into a dynamic business (manufacturing, retail, wholesale, and catering) that daily has us toeing the thin line between euphoria and despair.

There *is* no secret, or, if there is, it's still unknown to us, too. Our story works because it's actually true, not something a marketing executive dreamed up. Our product works because it's carefully made using quality ingredients. Our business works because we treat our suppliers, our customers, our employees, and ourselves with respect, trust, and affection. (And because we work our buns off.)

The business school students had polite, pointed questions: "Have you considered franchising?" "Can you identify your most persistent bottlenecks?" "Will you be taking on investors?" Nath answered them to the best of her ability, knowing that sounder, more experienced business owners would have spent time actually talking to each other about things like this. We don't, because whenever we come close to having thirty seconds to take a macro look at the business, the freezer fails and the van overheats.

So the monster grows, and we just try to keep up: that's our strategy. But we feel good about how, despite everything, we continue to be capable of keeping the most important things about our business intact: good local fruit, happy customers, and having fun with each other. Actually, wait: maybe that *is* our strategy.

late summer

people's pops

CORN
corn & blackberry | 76

CANTALOUPES
cantaloupe & tarragon | 78
cantaloupe & mint | 79
cantaloupe & campari | 80

HONEYDEWS
honeydew & ginger | 81

WATERMELONS
watermelon & parsley | 83
watermelon & lemongrass | 84
watermelon & cucumber | 85

FIGS
fig jam & yogurt | 86

ONCE AUGUST ROLLS AROUND, summer's really bursting at the seams. The basil plants are out of control, tomatoes are coming in faster than people can jam, can, and sauce 'em, and the melons have grown so prodigiously big that we can barely carry them to the van. The first cantaloupe and tarragon pop of the year is real cause for celebration.

Fruits such as tomatoes and melons may be easier to prepare than smaller fruits, especially those with noisome pits, cores, or stems, but their watery composition will result in icier pops with more shards. However, the more quickly you manage to freeze these pops (that is, the colder the temperature at which you freeze them), the tighter the crystals will be.

Another way to improve the texture of pops made from fruit with a watery composition is to add booze, which softens the crystals. Don't overdo it, though, because too much will keep the pops from freezing. Keep the proportion of booze at less than 20 percent of the total volume of the mixture. Although the texture of tomato and melon pops may be somewhat icy, pops made with these fruits are among the lightest and most refreshing that we produce.

. . . .

corn

Although veggie pops reside in the realm of the adventurous, they are gratifyingly stimulating and very refreshing. We advocate deliberate sourcing of your ingredients no matter what you're making, but because vegetables already have the odds stacked against them when used in desserts, corn pops should only be attempted with the sweetest late summer corn. We tested this pop with ears purchased in February and it was disgusting.

If you like our corn and blackberry pop, try a corn and fennel pop next.

cantaloupes

Okay, okay. We know we already anointed peaches as the epitome of summer, but melons, those buxom orbs with their waffle-weave shells and floral aroma, are without a doubt another high point. A table stacked tall with gorgeous melons makes us lusty like no other fruit.

To prep a cantaloupe for puréeing, cut it around its equator and scoop out and dump the seeds and fibers inside. Set each half on a cutting board, cut side down, and lop ½ inch off the top horizontally so that you've cut off a flap approximately the size of a circle made by your thumb and finger. Now get the rest of the rind off by slicing longitudinally, as if you had the northern hemisphere on your cutting board and were cutting the surface off each time zone around the world. Once you're done with both hemispheres, your cantaloupe is ready to purée.

Buy only cantaloupes that smell delicious even before cutting, because a scentless cantaloupe is probably a flavorless one. Along with the ideas in this chapter, cantaloupe pairs beautifully with lavender, hyssop, and tequila.

honeydews

Everyone loves to hate honeydew. That's because—let's face it—most honeydew sucks. To be honest, this pop can rehabilitate even a lame globe of honeydew, but if you make the extra effort to track down a tree-ripe melon, you might be surprised at how soft, yielding, and flavorful this fruit can be. Peel and seed honeydew the same way you would a cantaloupe (see above).

watermelons

The mixtures for these pops are so watery that the pops freeze into icy shards, but with watermelon, you just take that in stride. The great thing about watermelon is that, when it's in season, it's affordable and takes almost no time to prepare. We don't even bother to take the seeds out. In fact, we kind of like having them in there, 'cause then you can spit them out like you would if you were eating fresh watermelon!

figs

We really wish we could make fig pops throughout the whole month of September, but New York is too far north for local figs to grow any way but extravagantly expensively, and often they're not even that good. Our solution? Fig jam is a staple you can easily find even if fresh figs don't grow in your area.

But of course, sometimes we do think about just upping sticks to California, if only for the figs.

corn & blackberry

There's an intrinsic sweetness to corn that lends itself well to desserts, but when David saw a receipt for a bunch of corn that Nathalie bought at the market for making pops, he almost lost his mind. This made Nathalie very nervous. Would people think it was too weird? Happily, we sold out of all of our corn-blackberry pops in one day, and people were asking about the cornsicles for months. Whew. Nath really hates to lose face in front of David.

It is worth reiterating that you should not even consider attempting pops made with corn that is not at the absolute peak of its season. You will be wasting your time and the corn's. If the corn tastes sweet and wonderful raw, you don't even have to cook it. | MAKES 10 POPS

9 ounces (2 cups) blackberries

3/4 cup (6 fl oz) simple syrup (page 7)

Kosher salt

3 pounds fresh corn on the cob (about 5 ears), husks and silks removed

Purée the blackberries in a food processor, then mix in 1/4 cup (2 fl oz) of the simple syrup, or enough to make the mixture taste quite sweet. Strain the blackberry mixture through a sieve into a bowl or measuring pitcher with a pouring spout and discard the seeds. Divide the mixture equally between your ice pop molds, being careful not to drip down the sides (they should each be about a third full with blackberry mixture). Freeze for 1 to 2 hours, or until solid enough to poke without bursting.

Heat a large pot of lightly salted water. When it comes to a boil, toss in the ears of corn and boil for about 5 minutes. Drain the corn and run cold water over it until it is cool enough to handle. Using a knife, cut the kernels from the cobs. Discard the cobs. Transfer the kernels to a food processor and purée until smooth.

Transfer 1¹⁄₄ cups (10 fl oz) of the puréed corn to a bowl or measuring pitcher with a pouring spout and add simple syrup to taste, using approximately the remaining ¹⁄₂ cup (4 fl oz), until the mixture becomes quite sweet. The amount you use will depend on how sweet the corn was to begin with, so use your judgment and remember that the sweetness will dull when the ingredients are frozen. Strain the corn through a sieve with big holes—or don't bother to strain it at all.

Pour the corn mixture on top of the frozen blackberry layer in your ice pop molds, leaving a little bit of room at the top for the mixture to expand. Insert sticks and freeze until solid, 4 to 5 hours. Unmold and transfer to plastic bags for storage or serve at once.

cantaloupe & tarragon

Incredibly versatile, tarragon is one of our favorite herbs to mix into pops. Have a bunch of tarragon wilting in the fridge? Use it to bring pleasure to peaches, plums (page 68), nectarines, or watermelon. This pop, though, is a classic. | MAKES 10 POPS

1 cup (8 fl oz) simple syrup (page 7)

2 to 3 sprigs tarragon, or more as needed

1 cantaloupe, about 2¹/₄ pounds, peeled and seeded (see page 75)

Combine the simple syrup and tarragon in a small saucepan. Cover and bring to a simmer over medium heat. Simmer for 5 to 10 minutes, then turn off the heat and let rest while the tarragon steeps. Be careful not to heat the mixture for too long, because the simple syrup evaporates quickly, reducing the amount of liquid remaining. You want ³/₄ cup to ³/₄ cup plus 2 tablespoons (6 to 7 fl oz) to work with. Let cool. Can you smell the tarragon? If not, discard the spent tarragon, add a few new sprigs of tarragon to the syrup, and repeat the simmering process.

Cut the cantaloupe into large chunks and purée in a food processor. You should have about 2¹/₃ cups (19 fl oz) of purée.

Transfer the puréed cantaloupe to a bowl or measuring pitcher with a pouring spout. Strain the tarragon, squeeze it over the simple syrup to extract as much liquid as possible, and discard the tarragon. Add the tarragon simple syrup to the cantaloupe until the mixture tastes sweet and the anise flavor is subtly detectable.

Pour the mixture into your ice pop molds, leaving a little bit of room at the top for the mixture to expand. Insert sticks and freeze until solid, 4 to 5 hours. Unmold and transfer to plastic bags for storage or serve at once.

cantaloupe & mint

Another extremely promiscuous herb in our repertoire, mint has appeared in our shops alongside blackberries, honeydew, plums, watermelon, rhubarb, blueberries, apples, and cucumbers. We use a lot of spearmint and peppermint, but mint comes in a multiplicity of flavors, so you can get creative with other varieties, like apple mint and chocolate mint. | MAKES 10 POPS

1 cup (8 fl oz) simple syrup (page 7)

5 to 6 sprigs fresh mint

1 cantaloupe, about 2¼ pounds, peeled and seeded (see page 75)

Combine the simple syrup and mint in a small saucepan. Cover and bring to a simmer over medium-high heat. Simmer for 5 to 10 minutes, then turn off the heat and let rest while the mint steeps. Be careful not to heat the mixture for too long, because the simple syrup evaporates quickly, reducing the amount of liquid remaining. You want at least 3/4 cup (6 fl oz) to work with. Let cool.

Cut the cantaloupe into large chunks and purée in a food processor. You should have about 2¹/3 cups (19 fl oz) of purée.

Transfer the puréed cantaloupe to a bowl or measuring pitcher with a pouring spout. Strain out the mint, squeeze it over the simple syrup to extract as much liquid as possible, and discard the mint. Add 3/4 cup (6 fl oz) or a little more of the mint simple syrup to the cantaloupe, or until the cantaloupe tastes sweet and the mint flavor is refreshingly present.

Pour the mixture into your ice pop molds, leaving a little bit of room at the top for the mixture to expand. Insert sticks and freeze until solid, 4 to 5 hours. Unmold and transfer to plastic bags for storage or serve at once.

cantaloupe & campari

The slightly bitter flavor of Campari is a great counterpoint to the sweet innocence of cantaloupe. This is an adult ice pop, but if you can find a dock to dangle your feet over while you eat this, we recommend it: you'll feel like a kid again, albeit a very wise one. | MAKES 10 POPS

1 cantaloupe, about 2 pounds, peeled and seeded (see page 75)

3/4 cup (6 fl oz) simple syrup (page 7)

1/4 cup (2 fl oz) Campari

Cut the cantaloupe into large chunks and purée in a food processor. You should have about 2¹/4 cups (18 fl oz) of purée.

Transfer the puréed cantaloupe to a bowl or measuring pitcher with a pouring spout. Add the simple syrup until the cantaloupe tastes quite sweet. Now dribble in the Campari until you can detect its flavor. Campari is less alcoholic than most spirits, so this mixture can handle more of it, but it has such a strong presence that you want to be careful not to overdo it.

Pour the mixture into your ice pop molds, leaving a little bit of room at the top for the mixture to expand. Insert sticks and freeze until solid, 4 to 5 hours. Unmold and transfer to plastic bags for storage or serve at once.

honeydew & ginger

Good alternatives to ginger in this pop are mint, tarragon, shiso, and hyssop. Or, for something completely different, consider imitating the exquisite Japanese honeydew-and-cream frozen confection that our friend Steve Porto once made us taste, which we've been resolved to try our hand at ever since. | MAKES 10 POPS

3/4 cup plus 2 tablespoons (7 fl oz) simple syrup (page 7)
2 tablespoons (1/2 to 3/4 oz) finely minced fresh ginger
1/2 large honeydew or 1 whole small honeydew, about 2 pounds,
peeled and seeded (see page 75)

Combine the simple syrup and ginger in a small saucepan. Cover and bring to a simmer over medium-high heat. Simmer for 5 to 10 minutes, then turn off the heat and let rest while the ginger steeps. Be careful not to heat the mixture for too long, because the simple syrup evaporates quickly, reducing the amount of liquid remaining. You want 3/4 cup (6 fl oz) to work with. Let cool.

Meanwhile, cut the honeydew into large chunks and purée in a food processor. You should have about 2 1/3 cups (19 fl oz) of purée.

Transfer the puréed honeydew to a bowl or measuring pitcher with a pouring spout. Strain the ginger out of the simple syrup and reserve the ginger. Add 2/3 to 3/4 cup (5 to 6 fl oz) of the ginger simple syrup to the honeydew, or until the honeydew tastes sweet and the ginger is zingy and vigorous. If you like a lot of ginger, add some of the minced ginger back into the mixture.

Pour the mixture into your ice pop molds, leaving a little bit of room at the top for the mixture to expand. Insert sticks and freeze until solid, 4 to 5 hours. Unmold and transfer to plastic bags for storage or serve at once.

watermelon & parsley

When Nathalie and Dave were kids in Miami, Nath's family had a potted parsley plant that she would secretly pinch bites from, like it was candy. She did this so often that the parsley suffered, and her mom, believing the plant had become diseased, threw it out. Nath, still a staunch supporter of the herb, believes that parsley is a superlative palate cleanser and breath freshener (like mint), and deserves a larger role in the dessert world. Can this be its debut? | MAKES 10 POPS

1²/₃ pounds whole watermelon (about ¹/₂ of a bowling ball–sized watermelon)
3/4 cup (6 fl oz) simple syrup (page 7), or more if needed
20 leaves fresh flat-leaf parsley

Peel and coarsely chop the watermelon. You should have about a quart of watermelon pieces. Purée the watermelon, leaving chunks if you like, as long as they're small enough to pour into the molds. You should have about 2¹/₄ cups (18 fl oz) of purée.

Transfer the puréed watermelon to a bowl or measuring pitcher with a pouring spout. Mix the simple syrup into the puréed watermelon until it tastes quite sweet. Chop the parsley very finely and add it to the mixture.

Pour the mixture into your ice pop molds, leaving a little bit of room at the top for the mixture to expand. Insert sticks and freeze until solid, 4 to 5 hours. Unmold and transfer to plastic bags for storage or serve at once.

watermelon & lemongrass

Watermelon lemonade is a flavor of shave ice that we love. In this pop recipe, we use lemongrass to simulate lemon's citrusy twang. | MAKES 10 POPS

1 cup plus 2 tablespoons (9 fl oz) simple syrup (page 7)
1 piece of lemongrass the size of a pinky, thinly sliced
2 pounds whole watermelon (about ¹/₂ of a bowling ball–sized watermelon)

Combine the simple syrup and lemongrass in a small saucepan. Cover and bring to a simmer over medium heat. Simmer for 5 to 10 minutes, then turn off the heat and let rest while the lemongrass steeps. Be careful not to heat the mixture for too long, because the simple syrup evaporates quickly, reducing the amount of liquid remaining. You want ³/₄ cup to ³/₄ cup plus 2 tablespoons (6 to 7 fl oz) to work with. Let cool.

While the syrup infuses, peel and coarsely chop the watermelon. You should have a little more than a quart of watermelon pieces. Purée the watermelon, leaving chunks if you like, as long as they're small enough to pour into the molds. You should have about 2 cups plus 2 tablespoons (17 fl oz) of purée.

Transfer the puréed watermelon to a bowl or measuring pitcher with a pouring spout. Strain the lemongrass from the syrup and mix the syrup into the puréed watermelon. The mixture should taste lemony, refreshing, and quite sweet.

Pour the mixture into your ice pop molds, leaving a little bit of room at the top for the mixture to expand. Insert sticks and freeze until solid, 4 to 5 hours. Unmold and transfer to plastic bags for storage or serve at once.

watermelon & cucumber

The two most refreshing fruits to freeze into ice pops are watermelons and cucumbers (which, incidentally, are distant cousins). This recipe, one of the first Joel and Dave ever made, is the perfect antidote to a really sweaty day. | MAKES 10 POPS

$1/2$ pound cucumber (about 1 small), peeled

1 pound 2 ounces whole watermelon (about $1/3$ of a bowling ball–sized watermelon)

$2/3$ cup to $3/4$ cup plus 2 tablespoons (5 to 7 fl oz) simple syrup (page 7)

Purée the cucumber in a food processor. Transfer the puréed cucumber to a bowl or measuring pitcher with a pouring spout.

Peel and coarsely chop the watermelon. You should have a little less than a quart of watermelon pieces. Purée the watermelon, leaving chunks if you like, as long as they're small enough to pour into the molds. You should have about $1^{1}/2$ cups (12 fl oz) of purée.

Add the puréed watermelon to the cucumber. Mix the simple syrup into the puréed watermelon and cucumber until it tastes quite sweet.

Pour the mixture into your ice pop molds, leaving a little bit of room at the top for the mixture to expand. Insert sticks and freeze until solid, 4 to 5 hours. Unmold and transfer to plastic bags for storage or serve at once.

fig jam & yogurt

If you are lucky enough to live in a place where figs grow so profusely that you have to turn them into jam in order to use them all, try this recipe, which results in a pop with an amazing taffylike texture punctuated with little crystalline fig seeds. Store-bought jam works fine, too. Try not to use jam that's too sweet or the finished pop will taste cloying.

| MAKES 10 POPS

1^1/$_3$ cups (11 fl oz) fig jam, purchased or homemade

1 cup plus 2 tablespoons (9 fl oz) water

^{1}/$_2$ cup (4 fl oz) organic plain or vanilla yogurt

2 tablespoons (1 fl oz) freshly squeezed lemon juice

In a bowl or measuring pitcher with a pouring spout, combine the jam and the water until they are well mixed. Add the yogurt and taste. The mixture should taste tangy and sweet, with a gloppy texture from the jam and crunchy fig seeds.

Pour the mixture into your ice pop molds, leaving a little bit of room at the top for the mixture to expand. Insert sticks and freeze until solid, 4 to 5 hours. Unmold and transfer to plastic bags for storage or serve at once.

DISPATCH FROM THE FIELD

There are tons of things about our business that we lament not having adequate time to develop properly: an inventory system we can run on our iPhones, an automated payroll system that keeps track of our highly irregular hours, a more eco-friendly and attractive packaging solution. But the thing that most galls Nath is our shop's incredibly banal freezer display case.

Initially we were hoping to have real pops on display behind the glass, but that dream quickly died after the lights at the top of the freezer kept melting them. So eventually we whipped up a batch of wax pops and popped those in the case. They look okay, but still . . .

Nath envisions a world in which our freezer serves as the stage for a fantastical diorama, with scenes like "Ice Pops at the Beach" or "Ice Pops Hit the Disco." Joel jokes that the scenes should be true to life at People's Pops, a retrospective of our finest moments. Yeah boy. We can see it already. How about "Nath Getting Hit by a Car," "Dave Nearly Getting Mugged While Van Shopping in Harlem," "The Rhubarb Delivery Is Too Heavy to Unload and the Truck Has to Return Upstate to the Farm," or "The Fire Sprinkler in Our Freezer Explodes, Flooding the Entire Kitchen"?

Maybe depicting these scenes in miniature could bring us one step closer to being able to laugh at them. Is this art therapy?

autumn

CRANBERRIES

cranberry & apple | 92

cranberry, star anise & campari | 94

APPLES

apple & rose | 95

apple & salted caramel | 96

GRAPES

concord grape | 99

PEARS

pear, cream & ginger | 100

pear & almond | 102

pears with cognac | 103

PUMPKINS

pumpkin pie with whipped cream | 104

OUR SEASON STARTS WINDING DOWN in the fall, but there are still some Indian summer days when pops provide welcome relief, as well as great pops to be made with autumn produce, maybe to stash away in the freezer for the winter. After weeks of light and airy melon pops, it's a relief to bite into something heftier, like a pop made with cream or caramel, especially once the weather turns nippy.

As in the midsummer chapter, most of these recipes call for stewing or roasting the fruit. This softens the flesh and skins of the fruits and also adds depth of flavor. However, this step is not entirely necessary. Using raw fruit gives the pop a fresh, crunchy taste and texture that you might enjoy.

cranberries

Cranberries, that great American fruit, make great American ice pops. Fresh and frozen cranberries work equally well. Look for round, plump, very red berries with no bruises, and don't wash them until right before you plan on using them. Cook cranberries only until they pop, because further cooking turns them bitter. Think also of combining cranberries with citrus zest, pomegranate molasses, or vodka.

apples

Apples have the longest shelf life of any of the fruits in this book and are available year-round. While we tend to use McIntosh apples, we also sometimes try a blend—McIntosh and Pink Lady make a delicious combination, or a Granny Smith and McIntosh blend is really nice, too. Using raw apples makes for crunchy, brightly flavored pops, while cooking them down mellows them out and gives them a gorgeous soft texture. To refine apple pops even further, pass the apple purée through a strainer. And remember this little trick for better flavor: a bit of freshly squeezed lemon juice boosts apples' low acidity. In addition to the ideas in this chapter,

pears

We've used mostly Bartlett, Bosc, and Comice pears in the past, but any variety of pear will work in our recipes. Pears also function as a great base to combine with any fruits of which you have only a small quantity (soft berries, for example—think pear and blackberry). If you can lay your hands on quince fruits and know how to cook them, these recipes (as well as the ones using apple) can also be made using quince, although you'll have to tweak the volumes. Other wonderful "pearings" include cardamom, citrus zest, honey, star anise, and yogurt.

apples pair beautifully with almonds, honey, star anise, and violet.

grapes

Want to know what's great about Concord grape pops? They taste exactly like a grape Popsicle! Artificial grape flavoring is based on the flavor of Concord grapes, and Concord grape pops totally recapture that familiar childhood taste, although in this case it happens to be the result of terrifically ripe, real fruit.

pumpkins

If you want to cut corners, you can use canned pumpkin to make pops, but it's actually really easy to peel a pumpkin if you attack it after it has been cooked. Using fresh pumpkin is the best way to get that wonderful fall flavor, especially if you're lucky enough to have access to some of the very worthwhile heirloom varieties, like sugar pie pumpkin (also called sugar pumpkin) or Winter Luxury Pie.

cranberry & apple

Feel free to play around with the proportion of apples to cranberries in this pop; there's no need to be doctrinaire. We like cooking both of the fruits in this pop, which results in a lovely, very smooth texture. | MAKES 10 POPS

2 small apples (about 3/4 pound), or 1¹/4 cups (10 fl oz) applesauce

6 ounces (13/4 cups) fresh or frozen cranberries

1¹/4 cups (10 fl oz) simple syrup (page 7)

2 tablespoons (1 fl oz) freshly squeezed lemon juice

Core the apples (there's no need to peel them) and cut them into eighths. Place the apples and the cranberries in a heavy nonreactive saucepan and add about ¹/4 cup (2 fl oz) water, or just enough to coat the bottom of the pan so that the fruit doesn't burn. Cook over medium heat, stirring frequently, until the berries and apples are both soft, about 10 minutes. If the water evaporates, add a little more to keep the fruit from burning.

Transfer the cooked fruit to a food processor and purée. You should have about 13/4 cups plus 2 tablespoons (15 fl oz) of purée.

Transfer the puréed fruit to a bowl or measuring pitcher with a pouring spout. Mix in the simple syrup, adding enough to make the mixture taste quite sweet, and then stir in the lemon juice.

Pour the mixture into your ice pop molds, leaving a little bit of room at the top for the mixture to expand. Insert sticks and freeze until solid, 4 to 5 hours. Unmold and transfer to plastic bags for storage or serve at once.

cranberry, star anise & campari

With this pop we wanted to nod to the traditional pairing of cranberries with orange, because Campari tastes a bit like orange and also pairs well with that fruit. Spicing the mixture with star anise gives it a haunting warmth. Mission accomplished on all counts!

| MAKES 10 POPS

1³/4 cups (14 fl oz) simple syrup (page 7)
2 large star anise pods
14 ounces (4 cups) fresh or frozen cranberries
¹/4 cup (2 fl oz) Campari
2 tablespoons (1 fl oz) freshly squeezed lemon juice

Combine the simple syrup and star anise pods in a small saucepan. Cover and bring to a simmer over medium heat. Simmer for 5 to 10 minutes, then turn off the heat and let rest while the spices steep. Be careful not to heat the mixture for too long, because the simple syrup evaporates quickly, reducing the amount of liquid remaining. You want 1¹/3 to 1¹/2 cups (11 to 12 fl oz) to work with. Let cool.

Place the cranberries in a heavy nonreactive saucepan and add about ¹/4 cup (2 fl oz) water, or just enough to coat the bottom of the pan so that the fruit doesn't burn. Cook over medium heat until the berries are soft, about 10 minutes.

Transfer the cooked fruit to a food processor and purée. You should have about 1¹/3 cups (11 fl oz).

Transfer the cranberry purée to a measuring pitcher with a pouring spout. Strain the star anise out of the simple syrup and discard. Add the simple syrup to the cranberry purée until it tastes quite sweet and the flavor of the star anise is perceptible. Stir in the Campari and lemon juice. You should be able to taste faintly the Campari's bitter edge.

Pour the mixture into your ice pop molds, leaving a little bit of room at the top for the mixture to expand. Insert sticks and freeze until solid, 4 to 5 hours. Unmold and transfer to plastic bags for storage or serve at once.

apple & rose

This pop is at once simple and elegant, with a texture like pure velvet. If it were a sound, it would be a harpsichord, played on an expansive lawn by a lady in a long white dress. Be careful with the rosewater, though, because it can be treacherous. One minute you're in the flower garden, listening to the pretty tinkling of the keys, and the next you're drowning in a bottle of Chanel No. 5. Too much is too much. | MAKES 10 POPS

3 to 4 apples (about 1^1/$_2$ pounds), cored
^{2}/$_3$ cup (5 fl oz) simple syrup (page 7)
2 tablespoons (1 fl oz) freshly squeezed lemon juice
1^1/$_2$ tablespoons rosewater

Cut the apples into large dice (there's no need to peel them), then place them in a heavy nonreactive saucepan. Add about ^{1}/$_4$ cup (2 fl oz) water, or just enough to cover the bottom of the pan so the apples don't burn. Cook over medium heat until the apples have softened, about 10 minutes.

Purée the apples in a food processor (or push them through a ricer) and then strain them through a coarse-mesh sieve or colander. You should end up with about 2^1/$_4$ cups (18 fl oz) strained applesauce.

Transfer the applesauce to a bowl or measuring pitcher with a pouring spout. Stir in the simple syrup and lemon juice, then dribble in the rosewater, bit by bit. Be careful! It's strong stuff. Stop when you taste it, but before you get a flashback of your mom washing your mouth out with soap.

Pour the mixture into your ice pop molds, leaving a little bit of room at the top for the mixture to expand. Insert sticks and freeze until solid, 4 to 5 hours. Unmold and transfer to plastic bags for storage or serve at once.

apple & salted caramel

Holy moley is this a good pop. The flavor just keeps going and going, and the texture is softer than angora. Caramel pairs well with hearty fruits (pear would be another good match), but we like how this pop nods toward the old childhood classic on a stick, caramel apples. | MAKES 10 POPS

3 apples (1¹/₄ pounds), cored
¹/₂ cup (4 fl oz) salted caramel (page 59)
3/4 cup (6 fl oz) simple syrup (page 7)

Cut the apples into large dice (there's no need to peel them), then place them in a heavy nonreactive saucepan. Add about ¹/₄ cup (2 fl oz) water, or just enough to cover the bottom of the pan so the apples don't burn. Cook over medium heat until the apples have softened, about 10 minutes.

While the apples cook, make the caramel (page 59).

Purée the apples in a food processor (or push them through a ricer) and then strain them through a coarse-mesh sieve or colander. You should end up with about 2 cups (16 fl oz) strained applesauce.

Transfer the applesauce to a bowl or measuring pitcher with a pouring spout. Stir in the simple syrup and caramel. You might want to sit down and have a few spoonfuls of the mixture for yourself at this point. Remember to leave enough to make pops with.

Pour the mixture into your ice pop molds, leaving a little bit of room at the top for the mixture to expand. Insert sticks and freeze until solid, 4 to 5 hours. Unmold and transfer to plastic bags for storage or serve at once.

Working in pops means that our days require an uncommon vigor, an unabashed willingness to get our hands dirty, attention paid to putting out a good product and treating people well, and a belief that all of this can inspire social and environmental change as well as pleasure.

Ice pops effecting change? Yes, if you think about the tens of thousands of pounds of local fruit used, the hundreds of thousands of dollars circulating within the local economy, and the fact that we're able to employ good people to further these ends. Ice pops as pleasure? That comes from our customers, including regulars like the security guard at the Apple store, the pregnant woman who talks to her belly as she eats pops, the guy who works upstairs compiling statistics for Major League Baseball, the mysterious man who takes twelve pops home in a bag with him almost daily, the trio of chemists from the DEA lab around the corner, and the Brooklyn Flea contingent we see every week, rain or shine.

concord grape

If a cheatin' heart doesn't bother you, here's a little secret: you can use grape juice to make this pop, turning it into the easiest thing you'll make all month. We prefer using real Concord grapes, though, for their deeper, nontinny flavor, as well as the interesting texture their skins add. But Concord grapes have such a short season (and can actually be quite hard to find) that we thought we'd offer up the shortcut.

You can use other varieties of grapes to make these pops, but they'll be less punchy. But if you can find seedless grapes, you won't have to go through the trouble of straining them. If you're using seedless grapes and not straining out the skins, you'll need only 1³/8 pounds for this recipe.

Because strained grapes have such a high liquid content, the final pops will be quite icy. If this bothers you, you can combat the problem either by adding booze, such as 1/3 cup (3 fl oz) of moonshine, or by combining the grape purée with a fleshier fruit, such as peaches or honeydew, to make a combo pop. | MAKES 10 POPS

2 pounds (10 cups) Concord grapes
²/3 cup (5 fl oz) simple syrup (page 7)
2 tablespoons (1 fl oz) freshly squeezed lemon juice

Drop the clusters of grapes into your food processor; don't even bother to stem them, because you're going to strain everything in a minute. Purée very finely.

Stir in the simple syrup and lemon juice until the mixture tastes quite sweet and extremely grapey. Transfer the purée to a fine-mesh sieve held over a container. Strain very finely, so that only the juice gets through. Push hard!

Pour the mixture into your ice pop molds, leaving a little bit of room at the top for the mixture to expand. Insert sticks and freeze until solid, 4 to 5 hours. Unmold and transfer to plastic bags for storage or serve at once.

pear, cream & ginger

We can't figure out whether this pop belongs in the "warm" or "cool" category of pops (see page 5). The ginger's on the cool side, cream is cozy-warming, and pears are ambidextrous, depending on whether the variety used is crisp and refreshing, like the Bosc, or soft and yielding, like the Comice. Semantics aside, this pop is a flavor bomb, great in the morning at the beginning of the season, when it's still a little chilly and the sun is just coming up. We usually use Bartlett pears and cook them, but if they're really drippingly ripe, use them raw. | MAKES 10 POPS

3/4 cup plus 2 tablespoons (7 fl oz) simple syrup (page 7)

2 tablespoons (1/2 to 3/4 oz) finely minced fresh ginger

3 small or 2 large pears (11/2 pounds), cored

1/4 cup (2 fl oz) heavy cream

Combine the simple syrup and ginger in a small saucepan. Cover and bring to a simmer over medium heat. Simmer, covered, for 5 to 10 minutes, then turn off the heat and let rest while the ginger steeps. Be careful not to simmer the mixture for too long, because the simple syrup evaporates quickly, reducing the amount of liquid remaining. You want 2/3 to 3/4 cup (5 to 6 fl oz) to work with. Let cool.

While the simple syrup is cooking, cut the pears into large dice (you can leave the skins on if you like) and put them in a heavy saucepan. Pour about 1/2 inch of water into the pan (or just enough to cover the bottom of the pan so the pears don't burn). Cook over medium heat, stirring occasionally, until soft and half puréed, 10 to 15 minutes. If, after 15 minutes, the pears are not lumpily liquid (this will depend on the variety of pear you use), whiz in a food processor or pass through a food mill. You should have about 2 cups (16 fl oz) of purée.

Transfer the puréed pears to a bowl or measuring pitcher with a pouring spout. Strain the ginger out of the simple syrup and reserve the ginger. Add $2/3$ cup to $3/4$ cup (5 to 6 fl oz) of the ginger simple syrup to the pear mixture, or until it tastes sweet and the ginger flavor is zingy and vigorous. If you like a lot of ginger, add some of the minced ginger back into this mixture. Yum. Add in the cream and mix thoroughly.

Pour the mixture into your ice pop molds, leaving a little bit of room at the top for the mixture to expand. Insert sticks and freeze until solid, 4 to 5 hours. Unmold and transfer to plastic bags for storage or serve at once.

pear & almond

We love pear-frangipane tarts, with their big bed of pastry, tousled sheets of sweet almond frangipane, and pear slices spooning on top. It turns out those flavors meld equally well in a pop. For a boozy alternative, use amaretto instead of almond extract. Add it to taste, but use no more than ⅓ to ½ cup (3 to 4 fl oz). | MAKES 10 POPS

3 small or 2 large pears (1½ pounds), cored
¾ cup (6 fl oz) simple syrup, or more if needed (page 7)
1 tablespoon almond extract

Cut the pears into large dice (you can leave the skins on if you like) and put them in a heavy saucepan. Pour about ½ inch of water into the pan (or just enough to cover the bottom of the pan so the pears don't burn). Cook over medium heat, stirring occasionally, until soft and half puréed, 10 to 15 minutes. If, after 15 minutes, the pears are not lumpily liquid (this will depend on the variety of pear you use), whiz in a food processor or pass through a food mill. You should have about 2⅓ cups (19 fl oz) of purée.

Transfer the puréed pears to a bowl or measuring pitcher with a pouring spout. Add the simple syrup to the pear mixture until it tastes pleasantly sweet. Add the almond extract bit by bit and mix. The amount of extract you'll need will depend on the strength of the brand you use, so keep adding and tasting until you notice a subtle but detectable almond flavor.

Pour the mixture into your ice pop molds, leaving a little bit of room at the top for the mixture to expand. Insert sticks and freeze until solid, 4 to 5 hours. Unmold and transfer to plastic bags for storage or serve at once.

pears with cognac

A deeply warming ice pop (ah, the paradox!), this pop is a veritable massage for the mouth. As an alternative, switch the Cognac out for Poire Williams, an eau de vie made from pears. Pears squared! | MAKES 10 POPS

3 small or 2 large pears (1^1/$_2$ pounds), cored
^{2}/$_3$ cup (5 fl oz) simple syrup (page 7)
^{1}/$_4$ to ^{1}/$_3$ cup (2 to 3 fl oz) Cognac

Cut the pears into large dice (you can leave the skins on if you like) and put them in a heavy saucepan. Pour about ^{1}/$_2$ inch of water into the pan (or just enough to cover the bottom of the pan so the pears don't burn). Cook over medium heat, stirring occasionally, until soft and half puréed, 10 to 15 minutes. If, after 15 minutes, the pears are not lumpily liquid (this will depend on the variety of pear you use), whiz in a food processor or pass through a food mill. You should have about 2 cups plus 2 tablespoons (17 fl oz) of purée.

Transfer the puréed pears to a bowl or measuring pitcher with a pouring spout. Stir in the simple syrup until it tastes pleasantly sweet. Finally, add the Cognac until you can taste it, but not too much or the mixture won't freeze!

Pour the mixture into your ice pop molds, leaving a little bit of room at the top for the mixture to expand. Insert sticks and freeze until solid, 4 to 5 hours. Unmold and transfer to plastic bags for storage or serve at once.

pumpkin pie
with whipped cream

This is one of the last pops we make at the end of the season, and as soon as the weather turns even vaguely autumnal, people start clamoring for it. You can opt to whip the cream or leave it unwhipped. Whipping creates an airier, almost foamy pop, whereas leaving the cream unwhipped results in a more gelatolike vibe.

You'll get a better flavor from using whole spices, but if you have only ground in the house, use a scant 1/4 teaspoon of each and don't strain them out. | MAKES 10 POPS

1 pumpkin (5 to 6 pounds), or 15 ounces canned pumpkin purée

1/4 cup (2 fl oz) heavy cream

GINGERBREAD SPICE MIX

1^1/3 cups (11 fl oz) simple syrup (page 7)

1/4 teaspoon minced fresh ginger

2 whole cloves

1/2 star anise pod

3 allspice berries

1 green cardamom pod

1-inch piece cinnamon stick, broken into a few pieces

Preheat the oven to 350°F. Cut the pumpkin into 8 wedges of equal size. Get rid of the seeds and stringy bits (or toast the seeds and snack on them while the pops freeze). Place the pumpkin slices on a cookie sheet and roast in the over until soft, about 30 minutes. Let cool.

Meanwhile, to make the spice mix, combine the simple syrup and all the spices in a small saucepan. Cover and bring to a simmer over medium heat. Simmer, covered, for 5 to 10 minutes. Turn off the heat and let rest while the spices steep. Be careful not to simmer the mixture for too long, because the simple syrup evaporates quickly, reducing the amount of liquid remaining. You want about 1¼ cups (10 fl oz) to work with. Let cool.

Peel or cut off the skin from the cooled pumpkin slices (this is much easier to do after the pumpkin has cooked than before). Purée the pumpkin flesh in a food processor or pass through a food mill until it is fairly smooth. You should have about 2 cups (16 fl oz).

Transfer the puréed pumpkin to a bowl or measuring pitcher with a pouring spout. Strain the spices out of the simple syrup and discard the spices. Mix the simple syrup into the puréed pumpkin; the mixture should taste quite sweet.

In a separate clean bowl, whip the cream until soft peaks form. Fold the cream into the pumpkin mixture; don't mix too much, because the marbled look is really beautiful.

Pour the mixture into your ice pop molds, leaving a little bit of room at the top for the mixture to expand. Insert sticks and freeze until solid, 4 to 5 hours. Unmold and transfer to plastic bags for storage or serve at once.

shave ice

people's pops

ALTHOUGH THIS BOOK is basically about ice pops, the People's Pops story would not be complete without discussing shave ice, our second contribution to world peace.

Shave ice is popular in pretty much every culture where it gets hot, including Uzbekistan, Thailand, Korea, Cuba, Hawaii, Taiwan, India, all over Latin America—and, of course, New York City. Customers are constantly sidling up to our stand to share memories of the *piraguas*, *raspados*, snow cones, *bingsu*, *bao bing*, *golas*, *granizados*, and *frío-fríos* of their childhood.

Our approach to shave ice is the same as it is with our pops: take a classic crowd-pleaser and see what it tastes like when made with real, ripe fruit. We think of the ice pops and shave ice as being symbiotic products at our stands. First, while the pops are hidden away in a freezer, the big block of ice looks so stunning that it draws a crowd. Second, the shave ice takes a little longer to prepare and sell than the pops do, so it gives us more time to talk to people. And, finally, the production of the syrups for our shave ice dovetails nicely with our production of ice pops.

As you'll see from some of the recipes in this chapter, our shave ice syrups can be mixed with alcohol to delicious effect, and you can change any of the non-alcoholic recipes to include booze. These syrups can even be used in cocktails that don't involve shave ice at all. Let your creativity run wild!

the method

To make shave ice, we start out with a humongous block of ice (it weighs about 75 pounds) and cut away small flakes with a small hand shaver (easy to find online) until we fill an 8-ounce cup with ice. Then we drizzle syrups on top, usually for about six seconds. If the syrups are dense, we might add the ice in several layers, drizzling the syrups in between. If they are thin and will seep to the bottom of the cup, we might add them all at once on top.

If you don't have a shaver at home (or, for that matter, a huge block of ice), you can still enjoy these frozen confections, although without the eye-catching method. Make "snow" by whizzing a bunch of ice cubes in a blender. Because the cubes need liquid to blend properly, you'll have to pour some of the fruit syrup into the blender before pulsing it, meaning that you'll end up with a product that resembles a slushie more than it does shave ice. It'll still taste delicious, though!

As with the ice pops, we follow a mix-and-match philosophy for the flavors: if a combo sounds like it'll taste good, it probably will. Most of the time we opt to keep the fruit syrups and the spice or herb syrups separate, so that people can choose their own com-bination instead of being limited to already-mixed flavors, such as lemon-mint.

We tend to sweeten our shave ice syrups more than we do our pops, because drizzling syrup over ice dilutes the sweetness. As with pops, however, remember that the sweetness and flavor of any fruit fluctuates wildly depending on its ripeness, the season, the climate conditions, and even the fruit's position on the tree or vine, so adjust the amount of simple syrup according to your taste.

rhubarb & ginger

This is a great way to use leftover rhubarb juice, because cooking rhubarb down produces so much of it. If you don't have ginger in the house, think about pairing rhubarb with syrups made from cardamom, citrus, or cinnamon. | MAKES 3¹/₂ CUPS (28 FL OZ) SYRUP

1 cup plus 2 tablespoons (9 fl oz) simple syrup (page 7)
2 tablespoons (¹/₂ to ³/₄ oz) finely minced fresh ginger
1 pound rhubarb (about 5 long stalks), trimmed and chopped into 1-inch pieces

Combine the simple syrup and ginger in a small saucepan. Cover and bring to a simmer over medium-high heat. Simmer for 5 to 10 minutes, then turn off the heat and let rest while the ginger steeps. Be careful not to simmer the mixture for too long, because the simple syrup evaporates quickly, reducing the amount of liquid remaining. You want about ³/₄ cup plus 2 tablespoons (7 fl oz) to work with. Let cool. Strain out the ginger, if you like, or leave it in for a more gingery result.

Pour about ¹/₂ inch of water into a shallow, heavy, nonreactive saucepan and add the chopped rhubarb. Cook over medium heat, stirring frequently to make sure the rhubarb doesn't stick to the bottom of the pan and burn, until the pieces have mostly dissolved into a thick and gloppy purée, 10 to 15 minutes. Pick out and discard any bits that are still stringy (there shouldn't be many; if there are, keep cooking until the rhubarb breaks down some more). Stir the mixture to smooth it out (but it doesn't have to be entirely homogenous).

Transfer the rhubarb to a colander set over a bowl and let the juice drip out through the holes for a minute or two. Reserve the cooked rhubarb for another use (for example, ice pops!). Combine the strained rhubarb juice with the ginger simple syrup.

If refrigerated, this syrup will last for up to a week.

strawberry & vanilla

We rarely make strawberry shave ice, because the subtle essence of strawberries is so easily lost when diluted with so much ice, but the vanilla really helps anchor the flavor. Strawberry-lemonade shave ice also tastes wonderful. If you prefer, you can omit the vanilla extract and steep half of a vanilla bean, split horizontally, in the hot simple syrup for 10 to 15 minutes before assembling the ingredients. | MAKES 3¹/₄ CUPS (26 FL OZ) SYRUP

Just over 1 pound (4 cups) strawberries, hulled
1¹/₄ cups (10 fl oz) simple syrup (page 7)
1 teaspoon to 1 tablespoon vanilla extract

Purée the strawberries in a food processor. Stir in the simple syrup and then the vanilla, bit by bit, until the mixture tastes quite sweet and the vanilla is subtle but detectable.

If refrigerated, this syrup will last for up to a week.

sour cherry

This is not worth making unless you have access to fresh sour cherries, *not* canned sour cherries or fresh or canned sweet cherries. For the purposes of this recipe, any of the latter are a complete waste of time. If you want to try a variation, combine sour cherry juice with ginger simple syrup. | MAKES 3 CUPS (24 FL OZ) SYRUP

2 pounds (7 cups) fresh sour cherries

3/4 cup to 1 cup plus 2 tablespoons (6 to 9 fl oz) simple syrup (page 7)

Remove any stems from the cherries and pit them using a cherry pitter or a paring knife.

Pour about 1/2 inch of water into a shallow, heavy saucepan and add the cherries. Cook over low heat, stirring frequently to make sure the cherries don't burn, until soft and crimson and the cherries have released a lot of delicious juice, about 15 minutes.

Transfer the cherries to a colander set over a bowl and let the juice drip out through the holes.

Reserve the cooked cherries for another use (ice pops, for example!). Combine the strained cherry juice with the simple syrup until the mixture tastes quite sweet.

If refrigerated, this syrup will last for up to a week.

HOW TO START AN ICE POP BUSINESS

- First, check whether the laws in your area permit you to start making food for sale to the public in your own kitchen or whether you'll need to rent space in a commercial kitchen. (Your local Department of Health, Food Safety, or the Department of Agriculture & Markets are good places to start calling.)

- More than likely, you'll need to rent space in which to cook. Look for an incubator kitchen close to you, or approach businesses with freezer space and ask to sublet, assuming this is legal in your area too.

- See if you can snag a spot to sell at your local farmers' market or at sympathetic local businesses.

- Try to broker deals with farmers for fruit "seconds," blemished but deliciously ripe fruit.

- Start a notebook for recipe ideas and look for inspiration in desserts, cocktails, cookbooks, perfumes, and at the market.

- Don't spend money on expensive equipment unless you have spent a lot of time experimenting seriously with simple equipment and are sure you want to commit to this business.

- If you live anywhere where the winters are even remotely cold, think about the necessarily seasonal aspect of the ice pop business and make real estate choices accordingly.

- Steel yourself for long hours and hard work . . . and delicious fruit and happy customers! Remember to have fun!

peach & prosecco

This shave ice equivalent of a Bellini is absolutely fabulous at parties. For a PG-rated but equally delicious version, pair your peaches with almond, lavender, or orange blossom syrups. | MAKES 3¹/₄ CUPS (26 FL OZ) SYRUP

1¹/₄ pounds peaches (4 to 5 tennis ball–sized), halved
1¹/₄ cups (10 fl oz) simple syrup (page 7)
2 tablespoons (1 fl oz) freshly squeezed lemon juice
750-ml bottle Prosecco

Preheat the oven to 350°F. Place the peaches cut side down on a cookie sheet. Bake until the skins and flesh have softened, about 20 minutes. Remove from the oven and let cool.

Once the peaches are cool enough to touch, remove the pits and whiz the flesh, skins and all, in a food processor until very smooth. Stir in the simple syrup and lemon juice and taste; the mixture should taste quite sweet and like wonderfully ripe peaches. At this point, the syrup can be stored in the refrigerator for up to a week.

Don't open the bottle of Prosecco until you're ready to serve the shave ice or it will go flat. To serve, stir the Prosecco into the peach syrup, but watch out, because the mixture will bubble fiercely.

roasted heirloom pepper

When we were asked to develop a few recipes for the Brooklyn Botanic Garden's Chile Pepper Fiesta, Joel turned a mismatched passel of peppers into this really delicious, unique treat. You can use bell peppers or even spicy peppers—mix it up! The peppers, by the way, can also be grilled. Just make sure they are thoroughly cooked before you purée them. | MAKES 2 CUPS (16 FL OZ) SYRUP

6 large or 8 medium heirloom peppers, any variety
3/4 cup to 1 cup plus 2 tablespoons (6 to 9 fl oz) simple syrup (page 7)

Preheat the oven to 450°F. Stem and seed the peppers and lay them on a roasting pan. Roast until the peppers are soft and charred, 30 to 40 minutes.

Put the peppers and any cooking liquid in a food processor and purée very finely, until liquid. Stir in the simple syrup bit by bit, tasting as you go, until the mixture tastes subtly sweet.

If refrigerated, this syrup will last for up to a week.

lemon & mint

Lemons don't grow near us, but this shave ice is so delectably refreshing that we can't help but break our own rules to make this recipe. Lemon is one of the friendliest shave ice flavors for pairing. It marries beautifully with basil, cardamom, ginger, lavender, star anise, tarragon, or any number of other things you might have preserved in syrup. | MAKES 4²/₃ CUPS (37 FL OZ) SYRUP

3 cups plus 2 tablespoons (25 fl oz) simple syrup (page 7)

20 sprigs mint

2 cups (16 fl oz) freshly squeezed lemon juice (from about 10 lemons)

Combine the simple syrup and mint in a small saucepan. Cover and bring to a simmer over medium heat. Simmer for 5 to 10 minutes, then turn off the heat and let rest while the mint steeps. Be careful not to heat the mixture for too long, because the simple syrup evaporates quickly, reducing the amount of liquid. You want about 2²/₃ cups (21 fl oz) to work with. Let cool.

Strain the mint from the simple syrup, pressing it to extract all the liquid. In a bowl, stir together the mint simple syrup and the lemon juice, adjusting until the mixture tastes very sweet and refreshingly minty.

If refrigerated, this syrup will last for up to a week.

index

measurement conversion charts

volume

U.S.	IMPERIAL	METRIC
1 tablespoon	1/2 fl oz	15 ml
2 tablespoons	1 fl oz	30 ml
1/4 cup	2 fl oz	60 ml
1/3 cup	3 fl oz	90 ml
1/2 cup	4 fl oz	120 ml
2/3 cup	5 fl oz (1/4 pint)	150 ml
3/4 cup	6 fl oz	180 ml
1 cup	8 fl oz (1/3 pint)	240 ml
1 1/4 cups	10 fl oz (1/2 pint)	300 ml
2 cups (1 pint)	16 fl oz (2/3 pint)	480 ml
2 1/2 cups	20 fl oz (1 pint)	600 ml
1 quart	32 fl oz (1 2/3 pints)	1 l

temperature

FAHRENHEIT	CELSIUS/GAS MARK
250°F	120°C/gas mark 1/2
275°F	135°C/gas mark 1
300°F	150°C/gas mark 2
325°F	160°C/gas mark 3
350°F	180 or 175°C/gas mark 4
375°F	190°C/gas mark 5
400°F	200°C/gas mark 6
425°F	220°C/gas mark 7
450°F	230°C/gas mark 8
475°F	245°C/gas mark 9
500°F	260°C

length

INCH	METRIC	INCH	METRIC
1/4 inch	6 mm	1 inch	2.5 cm
1/2 inch	1.25 cm	6 inches (1/2 foot)	15 cm
3/4 inch	2 cm	12 inches (1 foot)	30 cm

weight

U.S./IMPERIAL	METRIC	U.S./IMPERIAL	METRIC
1/2 oz	15 g	1/3 lb	150 g
1 oz	30 g	1/2 lb	225 g
2 oz	60 g	3/4 lb	350 g
1/4 lb	115 g	1 lb	450 g

Published in the United States by Ten Speed Press, an imprint of the Crown Publishing Group, a division of Random House, Inc.,
New York.
www.crownpublishing.com
www.tenspeed.com

Ten Speed Press and the Ten Speed Press colophon are registered trademarks of Random House, Inc.

Library of Congress Cataloging-in-Publication Data

Jordi, Nathalie.
  People's Pops : 55 recipes for ice pops, shave ice, and boozy pops from Brooklyn's coolest pop shop / Nathalie Jordi,
David Carrell, and Joel Horowitz ; photography by Jennifer May.
  p. cm.
  Includes index.
  Summary: "A collection of 55 seasonal ice pops and shave ice recipes"—Provided by publisher.
  1. Ice pops. 2. People's Pops. 3. Cookbooks. I. Carrell, David, 1982– II. Horowitz, Joel, 1981– III. Title.
  TX795.J67 2012
  641.86'3—dc23
                            2011046653
ISBN 978-1-60774-211-1
eISBN 978-1-60774-212-8

Printed in China

Design by Betsy Stromberg
Prop styling by Alana Chernila

10 9 8 7 6 5 4 3 2

First Edition